GROW
YOUR
OWN

Published by Tin House Books, Portland, Oregon, and Brooklyn, New York

Distributed by W. W. Norton & Company

Library of Congress Cataloging-in-Publication Data is available

ISBN: 978-1-941040-58-4 (hardcover); ISBN: 978-1-941040-59-1 (ebook)

First US Edition 2017
Printed in the USA
Interior design by Diane Chonette

www.tinhouse.com

SAFETY WARNING:

There may be risks associated with the consumption of cannabis, and smoking anything is hazardous to your health.

Cannabis has intoxicating effects, and when it's ingested, those effects may be delayed by two or more hours.

Cannabis can make kids very sick. Store all marijuana products in a locked area that children cannot see or reach. Children want to be like their parents and the other adults in their lives. When you use marijuana in front of them, they may want to use it, too. You can keep them safe and healthy by not using marijuana when kids are around. If your child eats or drinks marijuana products, call the Poison Control hotline as soon as possible: 1-800-222-1222. Symptoms can include: having trouble walking or sitting up, becoming sleepy, or having a hard time breathing.

Cannabis may harm your baby if used in any form and at any time during pregnancy or while breastfeeding.

Cannabis can be toxic to animals. Pets that consume it can experience a range of effects, from lethargy to coma to death.

It is illegal—and very dangerous—to drive a motor vehicle or operate heavy equipment while under the influence of cannabis.

If you plan to use cannabis to treat a medical condition, consult with a physician or licensed medical provider.

This book is intended for educational purposes. Laws pertaining to the cultivation, possession, consumption, and sale of cannabis vary widely from state to state; please check your local regulations.

Understanding, Cultivating, and Enjoying Cannabis

GROW YOUR OWN

NICHOLE GRAF, MICAH SHERMAN, DAVID STEIN, AND LIZ CRAIN

TIN HOUSE BOOKS / Portland, Oregon & Brooklyn, New York

Contents

"Of course I know how to roll a joint."

— MARTHA STEWART

INTRODUCTION

THE CANNABIS WORLD HAS LONG BEEN THE DOMAIN OF DO-IT-YOURSELFERS. For decades, gonzo horticulturalists have swapped seeds and strains, good techniques and questionable advice. Our forebears developed something of a culture, almost an oral tradition; wisdom was passed along from grower to grower, the history of various strains becoming increasingly colorful as years went by.

In some ways, times have changed. The latest projections have the legalized cannabis trade eclipsing $20 billion in just a few years, and with that kind of money come the usual suspects and usual problems. (That's not to say there weren't serious issues in the past; black markets encourage bad actors as well.) The current era has been dubbed the "green rush." As with the gold rush before it, hordes of entrepreneurs have leapt at the chance to make a quick buck (and much like those bright-eyed miners, many will walk away with nothing more than a good story). But also like 1849, there's a certain pioneer ethos you can't help but admire. Growers are breaking new ground and making incredible strides. Some of the old spirit remains, and we think it's worth preserving. So in an age when deep-pocketed investors are vying to be "the Budweiser of cannabis," we want to encourage an approach that's a little smaller, a little more interesting, a little bit closer to the soil.

This book will give you the background knowledge you need to start growing, the concepts you'll want to comprehend when it comes to setting up your space and making adjustments on the fly, and it will walk you—step by step—through planting, maintaining, and eventually harvesting your bud. But it goes beyond cultivation. We feel strongly that a deeper understanding of what cannabis is, what it can do for you, and the various ways to enjoy it are just as important as lighting, airflow, and soil science. Our hope is that this book will serve as a valuable resource even if you're buying your bud from the neighborhood shop.

Grow Your Own is designed for small-scale growers; it's not a handbook for commercial operations. It's for basements and attics, sheds and garages, closets and tents. And while we're not afraid to get into the weeds when the material demands it, our aim is to make the information accessible and keep you from feeling bogged down in unnecessary minutiae. Growing your own isn't just a rabbit hole, it's an entire system of underground tunnels. We encourage you to find the burrows you're interested in and keep on digging.

Because outdoor strategies differ greatly based on your particular climate—and shift from season to season—we've focused primarily on indoor gardens. But if you're growing outside, most of the same concepts and instructions apply. You'll feed your soil just as we've described in Chapter Six, harvest and dry your flower just as we've instructed in Chapter Nine, and enjoy consuming your bud just as we recommend in Chapter Eleven. But conditions will vary based on where you're located. Your best bet is to familiarize yourself with the concepts we lay out here, then seek out local gardening resources for further specifics.

And that oral tradition we spoke of? In the age of the internet, it has migrated to the message boards. There's a wealth of knowledge out there just waiting to be pored over, and a great community of hobbyists and professionals offering advice and leaning on one another for troubleshooting. But, as you might expect, it can be tough to decipher what's useful advice from what isn't. Years of prohibition have made fact-checking difficult, and many experts grow at a scale that doesn't easily translate to small spaces. Couple that with the fact that there simply is no single correct method and the prospect of a home cannabis garden can feel pretty overwhelming. *Grow Your Own* will serve as a reliable starter kit—it'll get you from start to finish, and you can seek out expansion packs as you see fit.

⚜

As I'm sure we can all agree, the highlight of any heist movie is the moment it comes time to put the team together: the sexy, quick-cut montage that introduces you to the key players and the unique talent they'll lend to that last big job. In a bid to attract Hollywood producers for a *Grow Your Own* film adaptation—and, of course, to make you more comfortable with our credentials—we thought a similar sequence might be in order.

In 2012, the citizens of both Colorado and Washington state voted in favor of ending cannabis prohibition. While David, our master gardener, had been growing for decades, Micah and Nichole were living in New York, going down their own individual career paths; when it came to cannabis, they were merely enthusiastic customers. But the prospect of being a part of something from the beginning (legal cannabis for recreational use!) and having the opportunity to help build a business—an entire industry—from the ground floor was too exciting to pass up. After being introduced to David through a family friend, we started hatching our plans for Raven Grass, the organic-focused grow operation we now run in Olympia, Washington.

The idea was to put our various backgrounds and training to good use. Each of us possessed a different skill set. We thought we could use them to bring a new perspective and a fresh set of eyes to the cannabis world and its standard way of doing things.

Micah had long been working in the fields of architecture and construction management, and he was excited to call on that background to engineer efficiencies and streamline processes. When we first leased the warehouse spaces that would become the home of Raven Grass, they were nothing but empty shells. Developed with a dedication to energy efficiency, Micah's custom build-out is fundamental to what we do; likewise, his understanding of light, airflow, and temperature controls was an indispensable resource in putting this book together.

Nichole was working in the New York fashion world, designing accessories for J. Crew's Madewell brand and freelancing as an illustrator. She was drawn to the prospect of being a creative on the ground floor, helping to craft a new voice and a more compelling aesthetic for an industry that hadn't yet established one. Cannabis dovetailed beautifully with her interest in alternative medicine, herbalism, and nutrition; now her vision is apparent in all things Raven Grass—not only when it comes to our branding, but in what strains we choose to grow and how we engage with and help educate the community.

David has been growing for over 40 years—both here in the States and in Amsterdam. He has a deep knowledge of plants, an unwavering commitment to quality control, and a passion for new and interesting strains. With his custom grow mediums, organic nutrient solutions, and natural pest-control strategies, David brings with him the kind of wisdom that only comes from ushering thousands and thousands of plants from seedling to harvest.

Liz is our newest recruit. As a food writer and co-author of the acclaimed cookbook *Toro Bravo: Stories. Recipes. No Bull.* she has helped chefs translate their techniques and recipes for use in home kitchens. We see this book as a similar project, a way to take the principles and practices we've developed at Raven Grass and share them with DIY growers.

✹

As legal cannabis began to find its footing, we weren't alone in our excitement. By the time retailers first opened their doors, all sorts of entrepreneurs were fighting for market share—even if it meant cutting important corners. At Raven Grass, we took our time. Even for old-school growers like David, the legal (and highly bureaucratic) market created a steep learning curve; for novices like Micah and Nichole, it was whole new education. We wanted to be financially viable, but we also wanted to build a company that reflected our ideals. As we studied various growing methods, it was hard to ignore the waste and environmental impact. The more we noticed a reliance on automation, the clearer it became that we wanted to be a business that provided living-wage jobs (and one that sourced our materials from those that did the same). As we learned more and more about this special plant and what it could do for people, the harder it was to view the operation purely in terms of profit motive; cannabis's benefits—both medical and social—forced us to take a hard look at the relationship between compromised quality and bigger margins. In a new industry—particularly one that caused some level of apprehension in certain segments of the population—we felt it was critical to help set a high standard, to be an asset to the people and places around us rather than a burden.

Developing practices that we felt good about took plenty of trial and error and a tremendous amount of research. But not only are we proud of the end result—the cannabis we deliver to shops all over Washington—we're also proud of the way we grow it. This book is a chance to share what we've learned and to talk about cultivation on an even smaller scale. As the new cannabis culture comes into its own, there are a few principles and concepts we want to champion, both in our day-to-day work at Raven Grass and here in *Grow Your Own*.

One of the most exciting parts of this project was the opportunity to throw open the curtains of the cannabis world. We think a better understanding of the plant and its uses will help combat harmful stereotypes and misinformation. Growers—like many tight-knit communities—tend to lean heavily on insider jargon; while it may serve as useful shorthand, it can also act as a barrier to entry. We see *Grow Your Own* as an opportunity to push back on the secrecy and proprietary attitudes that are all too common, and encourage access for anyone who's interested.

At Raven Grass, we try to celebrate the diverse range of cannabis consumers and reach out to communities that haven't always been the target audience of old-school magazines and the male-dominated black market. We hope this book can do the same. We adore, and want to honor, certain aspects of cannabis culture and heritage, but we're aware that much of it was geared toward white male consumers. We're a women-led brand, and we embrace that both in our product choices and by marketing to women. At the same time, we want to be mindful that a disproportionate number of the people reaping the benefits of this new, legal market are white—as we are—while a disproportionate number of those incarcerated under prohibition are people of color. (A felony conviction typically disqualifies you from obtaining a cannabis business license.) We need to work toward justice and inclusivity, both inside and outside the industry.

The benefits of cannabis go far beyond getting high (though that is certainly a benefit!). We want to spread the word about the plant's various cannabinoids and terpenes, and how they interact with one another. While we're all for potent, THC-heavy bud, we make it a priority to offer a diversity of strains with a range of benefits, and we hope *Grow Your Own* will help readers appreciate the many nuances of cannabis and develop informed personal preferences.

Finally, we believe in organic, sustainable growing practices, and products that are both environmentally conscientious and physically beneficial. We do not use harmful chemicals or pesticides—which are damaging both to the planet and your health—and in *Grow Your Own* we'll teach you how to raise your plants the same way. Too many growers on every scale are wasting huge amounts of energy—either out of ignorance, carelessness, or because they've calculated that the margins work. Whether it's thinking critically about efficiency, or reducing your carbon footprint by making your own nutrient solutions and planting in local living soil, we hope this book encourages thoughtful, responsible gardening.

It's an exciting time in the cannabis world, even if it's an uncertain one. We don't know what direction the industry will take, how state legislatures will shake out, or what will happen on the federal level. Regardless, we want to seize this moment to help spread the good word to those who would benefit, and to provide a trustworthy guide for those of you who want to roll up your sleeves and grow your own.

Chapter One

A BRIEF HISTORY OF CANNABIS CULTURE

WE'RE LIVING IN A GOLDEN AGE. FOR THOSE OF US WHO LOVE CANNABIS AND are fascinated by the depth and range of its uses, there may never have been a better time to be growing. This is not to say we don't have work in front of us: we should be speaking out for people of color who are inordinately the target of arrest and harassment; regulating the industry's use of pesticides and other toxic chemicals; educating the public about the medical benefits of cannabis; and ensuring that patients have the access they need. And yeah, sure, we could use one more great Neil Young record.

It may be tempting to look back at the old days—the summer of '68; the pre-Boggs Act era; maybe even the Shang dynasty—and feel a twinge of nostalgia. And fair enough: those times had distinct pleasures and enviable freedoms. But look at where we are today. A large portion of the country can procure cannabis with a prescription, and a growing population can *legally* enjoy it recreationally. We know more about how cannabis interacts with our minds and bodies, and thus we can better manipulate its various qualities, isolating and reinforcing the aspects we like and minimizing those that we do not. There are more strains, more varieties of experience, and more methods of taking advantage of this wonderful plant than ever before.

Still, as much as we're excited to look forward, we appreciate a good sepia-toned, psychedelic-tinged flashback sequence. Before we dig into the cannabis plant itself, and the subtleties of how to raise it, we'd like to offer a brief history of cannabis—its use, its legislative battles, and the culture around it.

1450 BCE

HOLY TOPICALS

The Book of Exodus includes instructions for making a "Holy Anointing Oil." The recipe calls for 6 kg of "kaneh-bosom," which many scholars and linguists believe to be cannabis.

79 AD

PLINY THE ELDER WRITES A PRESCRIPTION

In *Naturalis Historia*, our first encyclopedist recommends boiling cannabis roots to ease cramped joints, gout, and similar violent pain.

1500 BCE

FIRST WRITTEN REFERENCE TO CANNABIS

While cannabis use surely predates recorded history—the legendary Chinese emperor Shen Nung is thought to have discovered its healing properties back in the twenty-seventh century BCE—we find its first *written* reference in the Rh-Ya, a fifteenth-century Chinese book of medicine.

1000 BCE

BHANG

A drink that mixes cannabis and milk, bhang becomes popular in India as an anesthetic and anti-phlegmatic. Soon, cannabis is being used to treat a wide variety of maladies.

1492

COLUMBUS'S BLUE DREAM

When errant sailor and genocidal murderer Christopher Columbus mistakenly arrives on North American soil, he brings with him a supply of cannabis seeds. The Jamestown settlers follow suit 120 years later, and hemp becomes an early cash crop.

1851
CANNABIS ADDED TO THE US PHARMACOPOEIA

Among the afflictions it is purported to treat: tetanus, typhus, cholera, rabies, leprosy, dysentery, alcoholism, opiate addiction, incontinence, gout, convulsive disorders, tonsillitis, insanity, and excessive menstrual bleeding. (It will be removed from the *Pharmacopoeia* in 1942.)

ERYTHRONIUM. *Erythronium.*
    The root and herb of Erythronium Americanum (Bigelow, *Amer. Med. Botany*).
EUPHORBIA COROLLATA. *Large-flowering Spurge.*
    The root of Euphorbia corollata.
EUPHORBIA IPECACUANHA. *Ipecacuanha Spurge.*
    The root of Euphorbia Ipecacuanha.
EXTRACTUM CANNABIS. *Extract of Hemp.*
    An alcoholic extract of the dried tops of Cannabis sativa—variety *Indica.*

1930
"MARIJUANA" USAGE SKYROCKETS

Not the substance itself, but the term. Cannabis opponents start using a variant of the Spanish word for cannabis, in order to stigmatize its "foreign-sounding name."

1783
SATIVAS AND INDICAS

In *Encyclopédie Méthodique: Botanique*, Jean Baptiste Lamarck separates cannabis into two subspecies. Describing the indica samples a colleague procured in India, Lamarck writes, "The principal virtue of this plant consists of it going to one's head, of addling the brain, to make one feel intoxicated enough to forget one's worries, and to give one a feeling of gaiety."

1911
MASSACHUSETTS OUTLAWS CANNABIS

A few short years before the Eighteenth Amendment ushers in prohibition, Massachusetts becomes the first state to ban the sale and use of cannabis, though many states soon follow suit.

1936
REEFER MADNESS!

Tell Your Children—a cautionary tale funded by a church group—becomes a sensation when exploitation film director Dwain Esper buys the rights and begins cutting in his salacious insert shots. The retitled *Reefer Madness* remains a cult classic.

1964

DISCOVERY OF THC

Dr. Raphael Mechoulam, a professor of medicinal chemistry at the Hebrew University of Jerusalem, identifies tetrahydrocannabinol as cannabis's principal psychoactive compound. (He later becomes the first person to synthesize THC.)

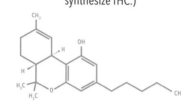

1970

THE NEW NORML

A nonprofit public interest advocacy group, the National Organization for the Reform of Marijuana Laws, is founded in response to the Controlled Substances Act, which classified cannabis as a Schedule 1 drug.

1964

INTRODUCING . . . THE BEATLES (TO MARIJUANA)

When Bob Dylan visits the Beatles in their New York hotel room, he is perplexed when they claim never to have smoked marijuana. Having misheard John Lennon's crooning on "I Want to Hold Your Hand,"—*I get high* instead of *I can't hide*—Dylan assumed the Fab Four must get stoned. He rolls them their first joints that day; by 1966's *Revolver*, they've gotten the hang of it.

1968

THE WOOTTON REPORT IS PUBLISHED

The United Kingdom's Home Office Advisory Committee on Drug Dependence finds that "the long term consumption of cannabis in moderate doses has no harmful effects . . . Cannabis is less dangerous than the opiates, amphetamines and barbiturates, and also less dangerous than alcohol."

1970

BILL MURRAY AVOIDS THE STRAIGHT AND NARROW

Premed Bill Murray, boarding a plane back to college, jokes that he has two bombs in his suitcase. When officials search his luggage, they find two bricks of marijuana. Knowing he'll be kicked out of school, Murray drops out, moves home to Chicago, and becomes the funniest man on the planet.

1974

HIGH TIMES

Founded by Tom Forçade and the Underground Press Syndicate, *High Times* is supposed to be a one-off, a spoof of *Playboy* that substitutes cannabis for sex (hence that centerfold). Within a year, the magazine has a circulation of 550,000.

1978

UP IN SMOKE

When Cheech and Chong release their first feature film, critics don't exactly go wild. History will be kinder: numerous sequels and spin-offs follow, and *Up in Smoke* is now regarded as something like the birth of stoner comedy.

1981

REST IN PEACE, LEGEND

One of the great musicians of the twentieth century, Bob Marley started smoking cannabis when he converted to the Rastafari faith. The sacrament had a significant influence on his life and music. "When you smoke herb," he said, "herb reveal yourself to you."

1971

NIXON DECLARES WAR ON DRUGS

How'd that work out? A year later, when the Shafer Commission recommends decriminalizing cannabis and removing it from the scheduling system, Nixon rejects the recommendation.

1976

DUTCH DECRIMINALIZATION

At first, this just means that the Netherland Ministry of Justice will cease to enforce laws against possession, but soon the system of "coffee shops" evolves, which allows for small quantities of cannabis to be sold by licensed retailers.

1988

THE CANNABIS CUP

The world's most prestigious cannabis competition, the *High Times* Cannabis Cup is founded by journalist and activist Steven Hager and takes place in Amsterdam (it's since expanded to other 420-friendly cities). The first champion? Cultivator's Choice Skunk #1.

1992

BILL CLINTON DIDN'T INHALE

And never tried it again. Honest.

1986

JUST SAY NO

The way Nancy Reagan tells it, the iconic phrase came about when an Oakland schoolgirl asked the First Lady what she should do if she were offered drugs; the truth is that it was shaped by a New York ad firm. As a piece of advice, it may seem simple and effective. But Ronald Reagan's drug war—for which the phrase became a rallying cry—was anything but, as we now see in the disastrous legacy of mass incarceration.

1990

CANNABINOID RECEPTORS

While scientists have known for decades that THC is responsible for many of cannabis's pharmacological effects, it isn't until Miles Herkenham—a researcher at the National Institute of Mental Health—discovers the cannabinoid receptor system that they understand why. Two years later, researchers discover endocannabinoids—the brain's natural version of THC.

1992

THE CHRONIC

Dr. Dre's triple-platinum record is widely regarded as one of the most important hip-hop albums of all time. It sells millions of copies, introduces cannabis ambassador Snoop Dogg to the world, and is designed to look like a package of Zig-Zag rolling papers.

2012

RECREATIONAL CANNABIS SHOPS

After Colorado and Washington become the first states to legalize recreational marijuana, hundreds of businesses open their doors and tax revenues far exceed expectations. (The following year, Oregon and Alaska rec shops follow suit.)

2016

DOMINOES FALLING

Voters in California, Massachusetts, Nevada, and Maine approve recreational cannabis; Arkansas, Florida, and North Dakota join the twenty-six other states that have approved cannabis for medicinal use. Experts project that by 2020 the national market could be worth $21 billion.

1996

MEDICAL MARIJUANA

California becomes the first state in the nation to allow medical marijuana, followed two years later by Alaska, Washington, and Oregon.

2014

AND THE EMMY GOES TO . . .

Comedian Sarah Silverman brings her vape pen to the red carpet, ushering in an age of cannabis couture.

2017

THE FIGHT CONTINUES

Not only is our new Attorney General opposed to legalization and in favor of mandatory minimum sentences, he once said he thought the KKK "were OK until I found out they smoked pot." We're not in the clear yet.

Chapter Two

WHAT IS CANNABIS?

THE RELATIONSHIP BETWEEN HUMANS AND CANNABIS HAS BEEN SYMBIOTIC, if not always easy. We've helped cannabis make its way across the globe, and have aided it in adapting to widely disparate environments. We've transported, bred, cultivated, and consumed it. In turn, cannabis has gifted us with its rich resins and fibrous plant matter. We've used it in medicine. We've used it for cloth and rope. We've used it religiously, ceremoniously, nutritionally, and—last but not least—we've enjoyed it recreationally.

Of course for most of us, our relationship to the plant is probably more informed by popular culture than by botany or hands-on gardening—we grew up seeing it in movies, hearing musicians sing its praises. Many of us have a rough understanding of a tomato plant just from watching one grow; when it comes to cannabis, we feel relatively removed from the growing process. In this chapter, we aim to give you the tools you need to grasp the fundamentals of this impressive plant's taxonomy, biology, and chemistry. Some basic knowledge will go a long way in helping you grow cannabis, and it'll make the process more enjoyable, too.

Federal restrictions have been a roadblock to serious cannabis research, affecting not only the plant's clinical potential but also awareness among the general population. As with anything relegated to the black market, there's plenty of anecdotal evidence out there masquerading as science. But as cannabis finds its footing—both in the culture and in the legislature—education, awareness, and appreciation can only improve. We hope that a book like this is a good step forward. So before you fill your pots and flip on the lights, let's explore just what you'll be growing.

Cannabis Plant Anatomy

SUGAR LEAF

PISTILS

CALYX

FLOWER:

Home to the plant's highest concentration of trichomes—the crystal-like resin glands that contain the plant's coveted cannabinoids and terpenes—the cannabis flower is what you'll eventually harvest, dry, and smoke. Clustered in **COLAS**—or bud sites—the flowers are made up of tear-shaped nodules called **CALYXES** (these contain the plant's reproductive material), **PISTILS** (those tiny hairs that collect pollen from male plants), and **SUGAR LEAVES** (named for their coating of trichomes, which give the leaves an almost dusted appearance).

FAN LEAVES:

The iconic emblem of cannabis, the **FAN LEAF** is responsible for much of the plant's photosynthesis and transpiration, and thus is crucial for plant growth and bud development. Fan leaves are connected to the main stalks by **PETIOLES** (small, stem-like transitions). They contain concentrations of trichomes, but far fewer than are present in cannabis flowers.

STALKS/STEMS:

The main stalk of the cannabis plant splits and branches out at sites known as **NODES**; this allows for multiple colas. While they are crucial to cannabis's growth, structure, and nutrient passage, stalks and stems contain almost no trichomes, so they're typically discarded or composted after harvest. They do, however, provide the bulk of the fibrous material used in hemp production.

COLA

FAN LEAF

PETIOLE

NODE

STALK

The Cannabaceae Family

While cannabis may be its most famous member, the Cannabaceae family includes nearly 200 individual species of herbs, shrubs, trees, and flowering vines. This includes hops—the very same used to make your beer—as well as hackberry and charcoal trees. Most grow primarily in temperate regions, and you'll recognize many from ornamental gardens.

Although taxonomic plant families contain multitudes, their members often have a host of similar traits, be it appearance, seed behavior, or their chemical features and medicinal properties. While there's not quite an academic consensus, many scholars believe that when Odysseus's men found themselves among the Lotus-eaters, it was *Celtis australis*—a Cannabaceae cousin—that left them dazed and distracted from their homeward journey. (Read Book IX of the *Odyssey* after a heavy joint and this may start to sound familiar.)

Most Cannabaceae plants are erect or climbing, and they are typically dioecious—that is, they are distinctly male or female, as opposed to being a single plant with both male and female parts. Many species within the family have similarly shaped leaves—either palmate lobed (think of an oak leaf, its veins radiating from a single point) or palmate compound (see the images of cannabis leaves on pages 30–31; their smaller leaflets each attach separately to a common point). The flowers are a humble bunch, usually small and not terribly flamboyant—this is because they depended on wind pollination rather than needing to attract animals or insects to assist them in pollen transfer. Beer drinkers might recognize a familiar smell in certain IPAs or other hoppy beers; this is because hops contain humulene, a particularly pungent terpene.

Cannabis Sexes & Seeds

The majority of the plant kingdom is monoecious. This means an individual plant has both male and female flowers. But almost all members of the Cannabaceae family are dioecious: each plant is either entirely male or entirely female. While this is largely true of cannabis, plants can turn hermaphroditic—this means flowers contain both female and male parts.

Only female cannabis plants produce flowers, so unless you're doing your own breeding, you'll want to destroy any males that emerge in your garden. Why so cruel? If a male cannabis plant's pollen comes into contact with a female plant's stigma, fertilization occurs. Once a female cannabis plant is fertilized, it funnels its energy into forming seeds rather than developing its flowers and cannabinoid-rich resin. When the ratio of resin relative to plant matter declines, you end up with lower levels of THC, CBD, and other active compounds in your bud. Long story short, when cannabis is fertilized, the quality of the flower goes down.

Finding seeds in your bud is never ideal, but it's bound to happen at some point. Don't panic, and don't get frustrated. Consider the occasional seed as a sort of gift-with-purchase—if the seeds are viable, you can use them to cultivate more plants. But if you find a male in your grow room and you've got more than a couple of plants at risk, quickly isolate it from your garden before it pollinates the rest of your crop.

As we mentioned, it's rather uncommon, but cannabis *can* become hermaphroditic or monoecious from time to time (you might recognize this plot twist from *Jurassic Park*). Generally, this happens as a stress response to extreme temperature drops, light leaks, or physical injury to the plant matter. If the environment feels threatening, it's a kind of emergency measure to ensure reproduction. In this scenario, the female produces male staminate flowers to pollinate its female pistil flowers. (In even rarer cases, male plants will produce female pistils.)

With a hard-to-find strain, a seedy plant may be seen as a plus. When David was cultivating cannabis in Amsterdam, one of his original strains, Stella Blue, was highly sought after but sold only as female clones. Customers with the right mind-set were thrilled when those plants became hermaphroditic, as it meant that they had the freedom to keep growing the strain from seed.

Cannabis Ruderalis, Sativa, & Indica

If you've so much as popped into a retail shop or dispensary, you're probably familiar with sativa and indica strains. These are the primary subspecies, the plants that produce the effects we cannabis lovers go looking for (and the plants you presumably want to grow). Ruderalis is the wilder cousin; because it's low in THC, it's rarely cultivated—though some of its physical properties can be useful in breeding hybrids. Sativas, indicas, and ruderalises evolved in different parts of the world under different climates and circumstances, so in their purest forms, they vary widely in appearance and effect. We find their origin stories fascinating, and some background knowledge is crucial for any aspiring grower, but when it comes to their distinctions and defining traits, we want to emphasize that those are a small part of a much larger story.

As most of the country is still saddled with prohibition, it's not surprising that the cannabis world is ripe with misinformation. For decades, language was oversimplified to accommodate a mostly underground market. The vast majority of consumers didn't have the luxury of browsing catalogs or display cases for a strain of their choice, or talking through their options with a well-informed consultant. And even as cannabis has moved toward the mainstream and options have become abundant, the lexicon hasn't quite caught up. People tend to say "sativa" when they want something uplifting and cerebral; they say "indica" when referring to a stonier body high. In fact, both subspecies can provide these experiences—they result from a combination of the strain, the user (emotional state, setting, and body chemistry all play a part), as well as the cannabinoid and terpene content of the flowers.

"Landrace strains" are those that adapted naturally to a geographic environment. They make up the building blocks of everything that came after. But cannabis plants have been bred and crossbred in a largely undocumented manner since humans first keyed into the plant's benefits. (There's never been the kind of terroir appellation system you get with, say, French wines.) As a general rule, breeders have cared more about breeding for traits than documenting plant lineage. The end result: it's difficult to find objective, reliable data on a strain's genetic makeup. Most cannabis you grow or smoke is a hybrid, even if it's not labeled as such.

Rather than using that binary approach, we've found it far more reliable to speak in terms of cannabinoids and terpenes. (We'll explore those subjects later in the chapter.) Whether you're buying seeds, clones, or flower itself, digging deeper into the particulars will ensure you get the strain you're hoping for. So with that very large caveat out of the way, it's worth looking at the three pillars of cannabis to see how and why they developed the way they did and what those traits contribute to our experiences.

CANNABIS RUDERALIS

ORIGIN: Central Asia and Eastern Europe.

PLANT SIZE AND APPEARANCE: Short, stocky, thick-stemmed, and wild-growing pure ruderalis plants (adapted to their harsh northerly environs) rarely grow taller than 2 feet. They're known for their small, shaggy, light green leaves. (They're sort of the Charlie Brown Christmas tree of cannabis subspecies.)

BUD APPEARANCE: Small, both in size and number, with very low resin production.

GROW NOTES: Because of their northern origins, ruderalis strains are highly adaptable survivalists perfectly at home with short growing seasons and extreme environments. They are hardy, insect-and-disease resistant, and fast maturing.

FLOWERING TIME: Varies greatly, but often a brisk 3 to 4 weeks. Most are autoflowering (plants whose flowering schedules are not dependent on light).

EXPERIENCE: Due to their low THC content, ruderalis strains aren't particularly popular in terms of recreational consumption (although they may have significant levels of CBD). In Central and Eastern Europe, ruderalis has been used in folk medicine to treat depression.

WELL-KNOWN STRAINS: Ruderalis Skunk, Four-Way, Ruderalis Indica, Taiga #2 (pictured). Ruderalis is typically bred with sativas and indicas in order to tap into its autoflowering, fast-maturing, and hardy traits.

CANNABIS SATIVA

ORIGIN: Equatorial climates—Thailand, Mexico, Colombia, Peru, and several regions of Africa.

PLANT SIZE AND APPEARANCE: Landrace sativas have tall stalks, leaves with long, thin blades—due to their development in hot, sunny environments—and sparse, delicate branches with long colas of buds (pure strains tend to be considerably lower yielding than indicas). They may be a lighter, brighter green, and some have pale orange hairs around the flowers.

BUD APPEARANCE: Airy, elongated buds that produce less resin (a tendency generally bred out of sativa-hybrid strains).

GROW NOTES: A pure sativa is notoriously difficult to grow and will require more time and attention (hybrids have been bred to counteract its trickier traits). If your garden has low headroom, you will need to bend and train your plants to grow out rather than up. Due to their warm-weather origins, sativas have a low tolerance for frost.

FLOWERING TIME: Typically 9 to 14 weeks.

EXPERIENCE: Often thought of as daytime strains. Highs are heady, energetic, uplifting, euphoric, psychedelic, and cerebral (and usually lack the body-relaxing effects associated with indicas). Sativas are used to treat depression, lethargy, PTSD, and migraine headaches and can be used for chronic pain.

WELL-KNOWN STRAINS: Durban Poison, Panama Red, Acapulco Gold, Laughing Buddha. Any strain with "Haze" or "Thai" in the name has sativa parentage.

CANNABIS INDICA

ORIGIN: Central Asia, specifically the Hindu Kush mountain range.

PLANT SIZE AND APPEARANCE: Due to their harsh and variable climate of origin, landrace indicas have evolved into short, squat, sturdy plants. They have hardy stems, wide leaves, and denser bud formations. The coloring of these plants is usually darker than that of sativas, with deep greens ranging from kelly to forest green, often highlighted with violet or purple hues.

BUD APPEARANCE: Dense and sticky. Because of their evolution in high-altitude regions, the plants produce extra resin as protection from stronger UV rays.

GROW NOTES: Pure indicas tend to be hardy and frost resistant, thanks to their mountainous heritage. Their buds grow in tight clusters that result in a higher harvest yield, but also make them susceptible to mold. Compared to their sativa sisters, indicas make for relatively easy tending—ideal for the beginning gardener.

FLOWERING TIME: Often as brief as 7 to 9 weeks.

EXPERIENCE: Indicas are associated with a relaxing body high. The effects are felt more systemically, less mentally, and can have a sedentary "couch-lock" feel. These plants are often used to treat chronic pain and inflammation, anxiety, tremors and epilepsy, and insomnia.

WELL-KNOWN STRAINS: Afghani, Romulan, DJ Short Blueberry, Ken's Granddaddy Purple. "Kush" in a strain name denotes indica lineage.

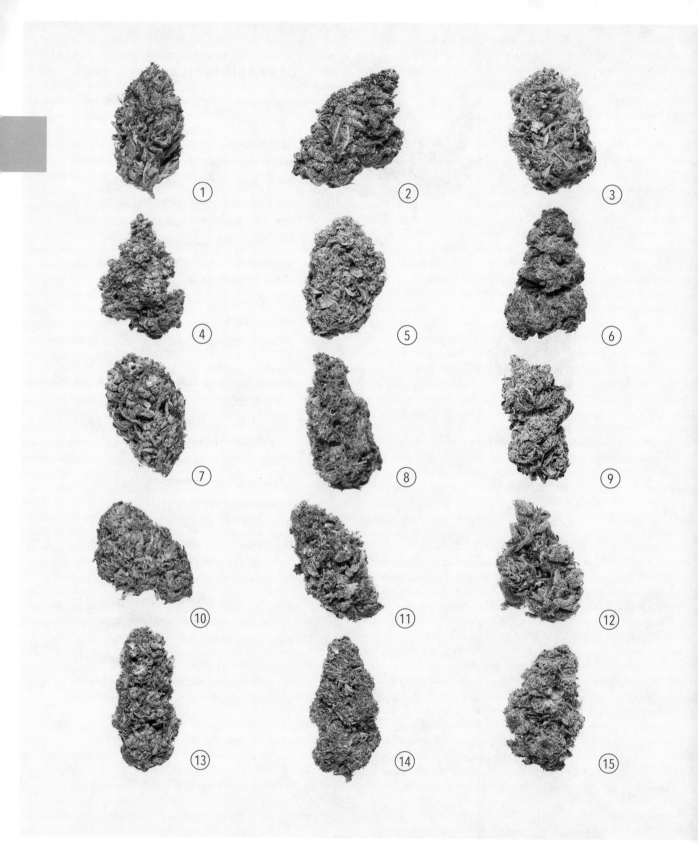

Strains

With any luck—along with a vigorous push from voters—the reign of the nameless bag of weed may be waning. If you're fortunate enough to live in a state that has ended cannabis prohibition, or at least grants access to medical marijuana, you probably have more choices than you can sample. Most shops have a whole spectrum of strain varieties—some you've likely never heard of. Depending on your "budtender," you might be greeted with vague, unhelpful descriptions, or you might be met with the kind of overdetailed profile that would make the snootiest sommelier roll her eyes. If you're not familiar with the jargon, or if you're not dealing with someone willing and able to walk you through the finer points, your visit can quickly become overwhelming.

But the tide is turning. More and more people—both inside and outside the industry—are becoming well-versed in the nuances of cannabis. Whether you're buying seeds, clones, or flower itself, shops are willing and able to cater to all kinds of preferences. Still, it helps if you know what to ask for.

As we've mentioned already, the vast majority of cannabis is some kind of hybrid, even when it's not labeled that way. And complicating matters further, strains aren't exactly stable. Usually when we talk about a strain, we're referring to its genotype, or genetic makeup. But if you've ever had a notably different experience with an old favorite, or if two Granddaddy Purple plants don't quite look alike, you might be dealing with different phenotypes—the observable traits brought out by the environment. It doesn't mean that that the genetics have changed, just that that there are variables in the way the genotype interacts with outer conditions. (Of course, the issue could also be that your supplier is playing fast and loose with the labels.)

Part of the fun of being a breeder is picking out the right name for your strain—usually it reflects an aspect of the plant's properties: its effects, taste, color, smell, or origin. Our new CBD strain, for example, provides physical relief (as CBD is wont to do) and a mental breath of fresh air; it relaxes the body and mind while still encouraging creativity and productivity. We decided to call it Frida, after the artist Frida Kahlo, "the heroine of pain." She was known for her ability to channel her physical agony and mental distress into some of the greatest art of the 20th century. We liked the idea of celebrating her life and work, as well as the inspiration she brought to so many of us. (The hope is that *our* Frida brings some of the same.)

We'll dig deeper into cannabinoids and terpenes later in the chapter, but first we want to outline a few important strains—listed, roughly, from sativa dominant to indica dominant—just to give just to give you a primer on your choices. Anyone who's made a desert-island list knows the anguish of narrowing down your favorites—our apologies to Silver Tip, Blue Dream, and ACDC—but we think the following represents a good overview of the touchstones.

ACAPULCO GOLD

ORIGIN

A North American landrace sativa hailing from Acapulco de Juárez, Mexico. The strain dates back to at least the late 1960s, and is still one of the most well-known and sought after.

FLAVOR/SCENT

Tropical fruits, caramelized sugar, and a little bit of spice.

APPEARANCE

Elongated brownish-gold or greenish-gold leaves; large flowers with rust-orange hairs.

EXPERIENCE

Long-lasting positive vibes. Some folks experience cotton-mouth and dry eyes from Acapulco Gold, but that's offset by a cerebral and generally uplifting buzz.

GROW NOTES

As with most landrace sativas, long-flowering Acapulco Gold is more suitable to outdoor cultivation (though breeders have crossbred it to create all sorts of well-known strains that thrive indoors).

FUN FACT

Often used as a benchmark for baby boomers talking about the old days. Over the years Acapulco Gold has had more pop-culture cameos than we can count, including several mentions in Cheech and Chong's seminal stoner film *Up in Smoke*.

DURBAN POISON

ORIGIN

An African landrace sativa named for the South African port city of Durban. It was first documented in the late 1970s, but likely goes back even further.

FLAVOR/SCENT

Strong lemon/citrus notes, with anise/licorice and sweet fruits.

APPEARANCE

An anomaly in the world of landrace sativas, Durban Poison produces buds that are well-formed, dense, and resinous with a moderate-to-heavy covering of light orange hairs and trichomes.

EXPERIENCE

Incredibly potent, with an immediate heady rush. Durban Poison is known by some as a "narcotic sativa" for the dreamy, stony undertones to its primarily stimulating and energetic high. This is a daytime, get-shit-done shot of energy and motivation. It can be a creative stimulant for some, but others—be warned—find it overwhelming.

GROW NOTES

While many equatorial landrace sativas are characterized as gangling, overstretched, or sensitive, Durban Poison is favored by growers for its chunky, even flowers and robust, dependable yield. A rewarding way for gardeners to cultivate a heady, potent sativa from a fairly hardy and easy-to-grow plant.

FUN FACT

Durban is Africa's busiest port, and cannabis enthusiasts have its commerce and culture to thank for Durban Poison's spread across the world. This strain is by far the most well-known African cannabis export.

③ SUPER SILVER HAZE

ORIGIN

Bred by Green House Seeds in Amsterdam, this strain has all of the true-breeding landrace sativas in its DNA, along with Northern Lights #5 and Skunk #1.

FLAVOR/SCENT

Sweet, citrusy, spicy.

APPEARANCE

Tall in stature with abundant, dense, resinous flowers.

EXPERIENCE

An uplifting, energetic, and long-lasting body high that's favored by medical marijuana folks as well as recreational users.

GROW NOTES

Super Silver Haze is best grown indoors (many feel it thrives hydroponically), but may not be ideal for the novice gardener as it can be a bit finicky. We recommend holding off on this one until you have a few crops under your belt.

FUN FACT

One of only two strains to win back-to-back championships in the *High Times* Cannabis Cup. (The other, Super Lemon Haze, is a direct descendant.)

④ JACK HERER

ORIGIN

Amsterdam's Sensi Seeds is responsible for creating this sativa-dominant hybrid, which crosses a Haze hybrid with Northern Lights #5 and Shiva Skunk.

FLAVOR/SCENT

Candy sweetness, with warm citrus/tropical fruit and sharp pine undertones.

APPEARANCE

Tall plants with large, resinous flowers covered in trichomes and, occasionally, pale orange hairs.

EXPERIENCE

A high-energy, potent, cerebral effect that can feel clearheaded or overwhelming, depending on the user. Typically uplifting, happy, and motivating.

GROW NOTES

Jack Herer is a garden favorite: it develops and flowers quickly, it has high yields, and it's moderately easy to cultivate. It's also a great indoor plant for those working with small spaces, as its branches grow upward rather than laterally—thereby taking up less of your floor space.

FUN FACT

The late Jack Herer—the strain's namesake—was a cannabis decriminalization activist and the author of *The Emperor Wears No Clothes*, a 1985 nonfiction book about cannabis history and its prohibition. This strain was named in his honor.

CHEMDOG/CHEMDAWG

ORIGIN

One of the more storied—which is not to say reliably documented—strains, this sativa-indica hybrid is named for the breeder who supposedly found these legendary seeds in a pound of bud purchased at a 1991 Grateful Dead show in Indiana. From there, the strain made its way east to New York and west to California.

FLAVOR/SCENT

Citrus and gasoline—Chemdog is one of the more pungent strains on the market.

APPEARANCE

Stretchy, medium-sized plant with copious flower sites.

EXPERIENCE

Potent, long lasting, and cerebral, but with heavy couch-lock potential as well. This is a strain that will *Get. You. Stoned.* In the world of medical marijuana, it's considered effective for pain management and as a sleep aid.

GROW NOTES

High yielding, fairly compact, and vigorous. Due to the density of the flower formation and flowers themselves, these plants can be susceptible to mold as the flowers develop; be sure to keep your canopy clean and manageable to aid in avoiding these kinds of problems.

FUN FACT

Chemdog has spawned many notable strains over the years, including OG Kush, Sour Diesel, and Stardawg.

GRANDDADDY PURPLE

ORIGIN

This cross of Purple Urkle and Big Bud, first bred in 2003 by the Bay Area medical-marijuana activist Ken Estes, is considered the most popular of the purple strains.

FLAVOR/SCENT

Smooth grape and berry notes.

APPEARANCE

Deep purple flowers and well-formed, hefty buds coated with a heavy cover of trichomes over bright orange hairs.

EXPERIENCE

Granddaddy Purple is both mind calming and physically relaxing. Often used medicinally for treating pain, stress, and insomnia.

GROW NOTES

High yielding, hearty, and relatively easy to grow. Because of its dense bud structures, you'll want to be sure you have sufficient air circulation and a clean canopy to avoid mold formation during flowering.

FUN FACT

Breeder Ken Estes became so frustrated by folks selling knockoff Granddaddy Purple seeds that he rebranded his original strain as Ken's Granddaddy Purp (though now the names are used nearly interchangeably).

SOUR DIESEL

ORIGIN

The lineage of this sativa-heavy hybrid remains disputed. Some argue that it's a sativa-leaning phenotype of the Chemdawg strain itself, while others claim it's a descendant of Chemdawg crossed with Northern Lights and Skunk #1. It became a sought-after strain in the nineties and has very much retained its popularity.

FLAVOR/SCENT

Citrus zest mixed with pungent gasoline (hence "diesel").

APPEARANCE

Thick buds covered in crystalline-trichomes, with coral/orange hairs.

EXPERIENCE

Known for its fast-acting, big burst of energy, Sour Diesel is highly cerebral and often used medicinally for treating depression.

GROW NOTES

Sour Diesel can grow very tall, so if you're growing indoors, be prepared to train it. It typically flowers late (in the ten-to-twelve-week range), but once it does, it's very high yielding.

FUN FACT

A very popular strain on the East Coast. When we lived in New York City, everyone who sold us grass had Sour Diesel (or at least what they told us was Sour D) on permanent rotation.

MAUI WOWIE

ORIGIN

A sativa hybrid thought to be first bred and grown outdoors in Maui's volcanic soil. It dates back to the sixties, but arrived on the mainland a decade later and soon became popular worldwide.

FLAVOR/SCENT

Tropical fruits, citrus, and earth.

APPEARANCE

Tall, lanky stems; long, large, and well-formed flowers; bright green with light orange hairs and a sugary coating of trichomes.

EXPERIENCE

Creative, uplifting, and happy. Potent but well balanced—an overall body relaxation accompanies its cerebral effect.

GROW NOTES

Unless you live in a warm, tropical environment, this high-yielding strain should be grown indoors. Because it comes from a humid climate and has an airier structure, it's fairly resistant to molds and mildews.

FUN FACT

Maui Wowie's introduction to the cannabis world is considered to be something of a turning point in THC potency—it usually contains 13%. Before Maui Wowie came on the scene, most available cannabis averaged around 8% THC.

WHITE WIDOW

ORIGIN

Introduced to the world by way of numerous mid-nineties Cannabis Cup appearances, White Widow may have been bred as early as a decade prior. This sativa-indica hybrid is a cross between a Brazilian landrace sativa and a South Indian indica.

FLAVOR/SCENT

Forest pines and citrus fruits.

APPEARANCE

Leaves are long and lanky, but the plant itself is fairly compact. It was named for its abundant white trichomes, which give the flowers an overall frosted effect.

EXPERIENCE

Big, spacey, cerebral, psychedelic high. White Widow packs a punch.

GROW NOTES

Easy to clone and best suited for indoor cultivation, but if you're growing outdoors or in an open-air setup, this is a good option for mild, temperate regions.

FUN FACT

White Widow has won numerous awards in Amsterdam and can be found in most of the city's many coffee shops.

CANNATONIC

ORIGIN

First bred by Barcelona's Resin Seeds in 2008, early on in the CBD movement. This high-CBD hybrid is rumored to be bred from MKUltra and G-13 Haze, though the breeders themselves do not cite its specific lineage.

FLAVOR/SCENT

Lemon, sweet grass, woody.

APPEARANCE

Dark green flowers with white and orange hairs.

EXPERIENCE

Ideally low in THC, with elevated CBD content, Cannatonic provides a relaxing body melt and minimal psychoactivity. Often prescribed for pain relief, migraines, and epilepsy. Well suited to more regular use as a medical supplement due to its very mild cerebral effects.

GROW NOTES

While Cannatonic is particularly pest-resistant, it is susceptible to mold and mildew. Resin Seeds recommends positioning your lights slightly higher than usual, as the plants respond well to a higher light source. If growing Cannatonic from seed, be aware that there are three known phenotypes: about half tend to have balanced THC/CBD ratios; some will be CBD-heavy with very little THC present; and a small portion will be have a high-THC/low-CBD ratio.

FUN FACT

One of the first well-known high-CBD strains to hit the medical community, Cannatonic provided a starting point for even more CBD-rich genetics to come (including ACDC).

G-13

ORIGIN

If you believe the stories, this high-THC, indica-dominant Afghani strain was developed in a lab at the University of Mississippi in the sixties, when (here's where things start to get hazy) the CIA and FBI teamed up to source the most potent varieties of cannabis from all over the world in order to crossbreed a superstrain. The new genetics that resulted were labeled chronologically, from G-1 to G-23. G-13 was selected as the cream of the crop. Somehow, a cutting was smuggled out and found its way into gardens in both the United States and Amsterdam.

FLAVOR/SCENT

Orange, apple, pine, spice.

APPEARANCE

Very dense, bright green flowers covered with orange hairs and a heavy dusting of trichomes.

EXPERIENCE

G-13 launches with a heady, creatively stimulating high that develops into a long-lasting—potentially lazy—body buzz.

GROW NOTES

Typically fast growing, but produces a smaller yield (which is why it is often bred with higher-yielding strains, such as Hash Plant or Haze).

FUN FACT

In yet another wrinkle of the theory above, the "G" stands for *government* and the "13" stands in for the 13th letter of the alphabet: *M*. That's right, you're smoking Government Marijuana.

OG KUSH

ORIGIN

Most believe that OG stands for "ocean grown," as this high-THC hybrid hails from San Fernando, California, but its genetic lineage remains a contentious discussion in cannabis circles. OG has also become one of the most recognized "name brands" in cannabis history.

FLAVOR/SCENT

Citrus, fuel, florals, soap.

APPEARANCE

Medium height and yield with compact, dense flowers.

EXPERIENCE

A heavy, euphoric, knockdown stony effect that may make it difficult to leave the couch. OG Kush is often used to treat depression, chronic stress, anxiety, and sleep disorders.

GROW NOTES

While OG Kush can stretch out in vegetative growth, it still makes for a good indoor strain due to its medium height and yield.

FUN FACT

OG Kush is one of the most ubiquitous cannabis lineages on the West Coast, and its naming structure has led to some classic combinations: Charlie Sheen OG, Mr. Miyagi OG, Sex OG, White Fire Alien OG, White Girl OG, Chuck Norris OG, Evel Knievel OG, Zombie Killer OG, Bob Saget OG, and Brain Damage OG. (The list goes on considerably.)

BLUEBERRY

ORIGIN

This indica-dominant hybrid—a mix of Thai, Chocolate Thai, Afghan, and Oaxacan genetics—was created in the 1970s by legendary Oregon breeder DJ Short. In an interview with Portland's *Willamette Week*, Short's son revealed that the strain came from pollinating female sativas with male indicas (most breeders at the time were doing the opposite). After much experimenting, he landed on the phenotype we know and love today.

FLAVOR/SCENT

Purple fruits in general, but as the name suggests, it has an unmistakable blueberry aroma and flavor.

APPEARANCE

Plants are usually on the short side, but may stretch to be medium-tall; the flowers are on the larger side, sticky with resin, and have a purple-blue coloring.

EXPERIENCE

Relaxing for the body, with an incredibly mellowing head-effect.

GROW NOTES

Versatile and vigorous, both indoors and outdoors.

FUN FACT

Blueberry won Best Indica at the 2000 Cannabis Cup, and has left its mark on the cannabis world by lending its fruity flavors to potent crosses such as Blueberry Trainwreck.

HINDU KUSH

ORIGIN

This landrace indica is named for its place of origin—the Hindu Kush mountains that span Afghanistan and Pakistan.

FLAVOR/SCENT

Spicy, citrusy, musky, incense-like.

APPEARANCE

The plant itself is compact, deep green, and somewhat conical; its leaves are wide and its flowers small and dense.

EXPERIENCE

Strong buzz known for inducing couch-lock, partnered with a mellow, contemplative mental state. Highly regarded in the medical marijuana community for its therapeutic attributes. Often cultivated for hash.

GROW NOTES

Medium to high yielding, short flowering, and easy to grow.

FUN FACT

The Hindu Kush region has long been regarded as the best in the world for hash, thanks largely to this landrace strain. While the strain has been a local staple for centuries, Hindu Kush only became popular in the US in the sixties and seventies, when travelers of a route known as the "hippie trail" started to bring seeds back to the states.

AFGHANI NO. 1

ORIGIN

A legendary landrace indica from the Western Himalayas.

FLAVOR/SCENT

Earthy; notes of musk, fuel, and spice.

APPEARANCE

Large, strong stems and sizeable, incredibly resinous flowers.

EXPERIENCE

Sedative and often narcotic high.

GROW NOTES

Vigorous, fast growing, and known for its dense, resin-heavy flowers. Lots of bang for your buck, and a good choice for a beginner strain.

FUN FACT

Like Hindu Kush, Afghani No. 1 is favored by hash producers due to its heavy resin production. This strain has often been used by breeders for its heartiness and high yields. (Its genetics have led to Northern Lights, Blueberry, and Sour Diesel.)

Cannabinoids & the Endocannabinoid System

While much of *Grow Your Own* is dedicated to questions of *how*, we think it's just as important to linger on questions of *why*. Namely: Why does cannabis produce the effects that it does? Why does inhaling and ingesting it produce that particular experience we've come to love? The answer: cannabinoids, the active chemical compounds found in cannabis (primarily in the resin glands of the flowers). The most well-known are tetrahydrocannabinol (THC) and cannabidiol (CBD), but scientists have identified more than 80 of these unique compounds. They work in tandem with the body's endocannabinoid system—basically, a group of chemical receptors found in the brains and nervous systems of mammals (our bodies naturally produce cannabinoids similar to those found in cannabis). These receptors are tied to a number of physiological processes—pretty much everything you associate with cannabis: mood, appetite, memory, pain sensations, and psychoactive perception. CB1 receptors, which are responsible for those psychoactive properties, are mostly found on nerve cells in the brain and spinal cord. CB2 receptors—which are responsible for many of the benefits we experience physically, such as anti-inflammation—are located in the gut, spleen, liver, heart, kidneys, bones, blood vessels, lymph cells, endocrine glands, and reproductive organs.

When you inhale smoke or vapor, the cannabinoids pass through the lining of your lungs and enter your bloodstream. (When you *ingest* cannabis, the cannabinoids must first pass through your stomach and intestines, hence the delayed high you might have experienced with edibles.) Eventually the cannabinoids reach your brain and nervous system, bind to the endocannabinoid receptors, and initiate the various effects previously mentioned.

But the individual cannabinoids are working not only with your brain and nervous system, they're working with each other as well. Each cannabinoid impacts the way another affects you. You're orchestrating different chemical reactions within your body, and the unique fingerprint of cannabinoids and body chemistry is what makes for varied and nuanced experiences. CBD might dampen your psychoactive response to THC; THCV might make the high from THC come on faster. This is commonly known as "the entourage effect," and might explain why synthetic THC (such as Marinol) has never quite replicated the original. We can reproduce the individual cannabinoids, but with natural cannabis, the result is greater than the sum of its parts.

There's still much to learn about the way cannabinoids interact with our brain chemistry, and it's widely believed that we've seen only the tip of the iceberg in terms of their medical uses. But for anyone interested in growing this marvelous plant, or tapping into its benefits—both recreational and therapeutic—a crash course in the most common cannabinoids is a must.

Breaking Down CBD

While tetrahydrocannabinol (THC) is primarily associated with the psychoactive effects of cannabis, the other dominant cannabinoid, CBD, affects the physical without producing mind-altering experiences. CBD first gained national attention when a young girl named Charlotte Figi was suffering from life-threatening seizures brought on by Dravet syndrome. By the time she was five years old, Charlotte was experiencing an average of 300 seizures every month; she lost the ability to talk, walk, and eat. As a potential treatment, doctors prescribed a high-CBD tincture, and shortly thereafter Charlotte's seizures had reduced dramatically. The first strain that Charlotte was given was called R4, but soon after, a pair of growers in Colorado—the Stanley brothers—bred a high-CBD strain specifically for her: Charlotte's Web.

Many scientists purport that CBD quiets the electrical activity in the brain that causes seizures. But it's also commonly prescribed for anxiety, pain, inflammation, Crohn's disease, multiple sclerosis, and PTSD. Some well-known CBD strains—in addition to Charlotte's Web—include Cannatonic, ACDC, Harlequin, and Sour Tsunami.

These days, high-CBD strains are becoming popular on the recreational market as well. Those who enjoy the physical relaxation cannabis can provide but who don't want the mind-altering effects, are discovering this wonderful alternative; we've certainly noticed an uptick in demand. The high tends to be more clearheaded, and there's less of a tendency toward couch-lock, which usually accompanies strains touted for relaxation and pain relief.

In most recreational markets, strains with 20% THC content are considered high potency. CBD content tends to range lower, with the strongest strains hitting the low twenties and anything over 4% being regarded as notably potent.

THERAPEUTIC PROPERTIES OF CANNABINOIDS

RAW

CBG-A
Analgesic
Anti-Inflammatory

THC-A
Anti-Inflammatory
Anti-Spasmodic

CBD-A
Anti-Inflammatory

CBC-A
Anti-Fungal
Anti-Inflammatory

CBGV-A
Anti-Inflammatory

THCV-A
Anti-Inflammatory

CBDV-A
Anti-Inflammatory

CBCV-A
Anti-Inflammatory

HEATED

CBG
Analgesic
Anti-Bacterial
Anti-Depressant
Anti-Fungal
Bone Stimulant

THCV
Anti-Convulsive
Anti-Inflammatory
Appetite Suppressant
Bone Stimulant
Neuroprotective

CBD
Analgesic
Anti-Anxiety
Anti-Bacterial
Anti-Convulsive
Anti-Depressant
Anti-Emetic
Anti-Inflammatory
Anti-Insomnia
Anti-Ischemic
Anti-Pyschotic
Bone Stimulant
Immunosuppressive
Neuroprotective

Δ9-THC
Analgesic
Anti-Bacterial
Anti-Inflammatory
Anti-Spasmodic
Appetite Stimulant
Bronchodilator
Neuroprotective

CBDV
Anti-Convulsive
Bone Stimulant

CBC
Analgesic
Anti-Bacterial
Anti-Depressant
Anti-Fungal
Anti-Inflammatory
Anti-Insomnia
Bone Stimulant

AGED

Δ8-THC
Anti-Anxiety
Anti-Emetic

CBN
Analgesic
Anti-Bacterial
Anti-Convulsive
Anti-Inflammatory

CBL
Unknown

CBL-A
Anti-Inflammatory

FLOWCHART FOR CANNABINOID SYNTHESIS

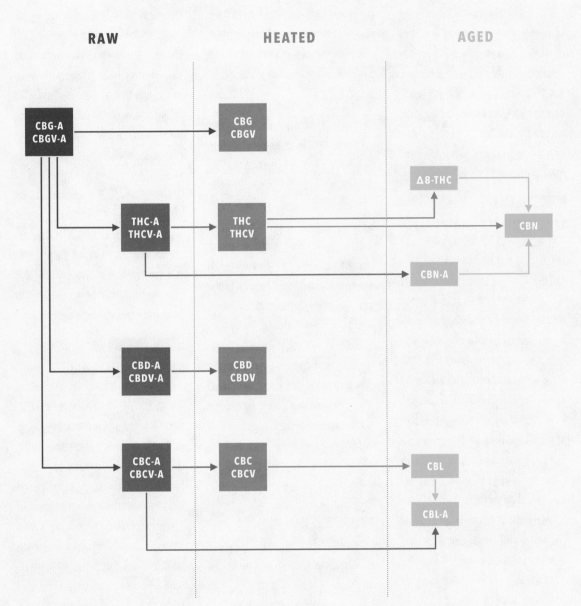

THC

TETRAHYDROCANNABINOL

The principal psychoactive compound in cannabis, THC produces a variety of effects, including the cerebral ones most often associated with this plant. But THC also has many therapeutic benefits. It's been known to treat pain, ease nausea, induce hunger in patients who lack appetite, and help in the treatment of Attention Deficit Disorder.

THC-A

TETRAHYDROCANNABINOLIC ACID

THC-A is an acid cannabinoid, which—for those of us who opted out of O-Chem—means it is nonactivated THC. While the plant is alive and growing, most of its cannabinoids are in acid form, and thus are nonpsychoactive. In order to be activated, THC-A must go through a process called *decarboxylation*. Technically, this is the removal of a carbon atom from the chain; practically, it just means applying heat. If you're smoking, your lighter or hemp wick will do the trick. If you're vaporizing, your battery will do that work and, often, you'll have a little more control over the temperature and can tweak the results. (We go into depth about decarbing for edibles on page 192.)

THC-A is typically the most abundant cannabinoid in modern-bred cannabis. Its purported therapeutic benefits are relatively new and have yet to be studied in great depth, but evidence is mounting for its positive effects, particularly in the treatment of pain, inflammation, and spasticity.

THCV

TETRAHYDROCANNABIVARIN

Similar to THC in its molecular structure, THCV is likewise psychoactive, but provides a number of its own benefits and effects. It's often referred to as "skinny pot" since it tends to act as an appetite suppressant. It creates an immediate head rush, a burst of energy, and typically decreases anxiety. In the medical sphere, it's currently being considered for diabetes (as it may help regulate blood sugar levels), osteoporosis (it's thought to stimulate the growth of bone cells), and symptoms related to Alzheimer's disease. It's commonly found in African landrace sativas, so if you're interested in THCV, look for Durban Poison, Malawi Gold, or a hybrid that uses their genetics.

CBD

CANNABIDIOL

We discussed CBD strains earlier in the chapter, but it's worth digging into the cannabinoid itself. Like THC, CBD binds itself to our CB1 receptors. But where THC connects to the *orthosteric* binding site, which activates psychoactive effects, CBD connects to the *allosteric* binding site, which modulates them. In the simplest of terms, CBD changes the way THC affects the body by reducing its psychoactivity while preserving its therapeutic effects. CBD is antispasmodic, anti-inflammatory, helps lower blood sugar (aiding in diabetes management), and has great stress-reducing and calming effects.

In addition to the specialty strains we've discussed, CBD is also found in industrial hemp, usually in levels of approximately 2% of its dry weight. (We still recommend cultivating cannabis at home rather than hemp, based on its yield and growing conditions.)

CBD-A

CANNABIDIOLIC ACID

Just like the process of converting THC-A to THC, CBD-A becomes CBD when heated up and decarboxylated. Research on nonpsychoactive CBD-A is still in its infancy, but it appears to have anti-inflammatory benefits and has shown promise as an inhibitor of cancer-cell growth. Historically, CBD-A has been found in higher concentrations in ruderalis plants, but more recently, many hybrids have been bred specifically for higher levels.

CBN

CANNABINOL

When THC is exposed to oxygen and high temperatures it gradually converts to CBN. It's still psychoactive—though to a lesser extent than its cannabinoid forebear—but is known for its strong sedative effects. While it's a product of oxidation, that's not to suggest it doesn't have its own benefits: for pain relief and anti-inflammation, and as a sleep aid and appetite stimulant. In general, heavy indica strains have higher levels of CBN than heavy sativa strains. That said, it's easy to unwittingly convert a good amount of the psychoactive THC into the lulling CBN, either by improperly storing your cannabis or by applying too much heat while making edibles. (We'll go into greater detail on this front in Chapter Twelve.)

CBG

CANNABIGEROL

CBG is a nonpsychoactive cannabinoid—cannabis typically contains only trace amounts—that is known to block the psychoactive effects of THC. Recent medical research has celebrated CBG as a rare neurogenic compound found to be particularly helpful in the development and growth of brain cells. Many cannabinoids—including THC-A and CBD-A—start off as CBG, but enzymes in the cannabis plant convert them into their final forms. Studies are currently being conducted that explore CBG's potential in treating anxiety and glaucoma and inhibiting tumor growth.

CBC

CANNABICHROMENE

Although very little serious research has been published regarding this little-understood nonpsychoactive cannabinoid, it's been touted as antibacterial, an analgesic, and anti-inflammatory; current research suggests it has potential in slowing tumor growth and combating cancer cells, as well as reducing anxiety and stress.

CANNABIS FLAVOR WHEEL

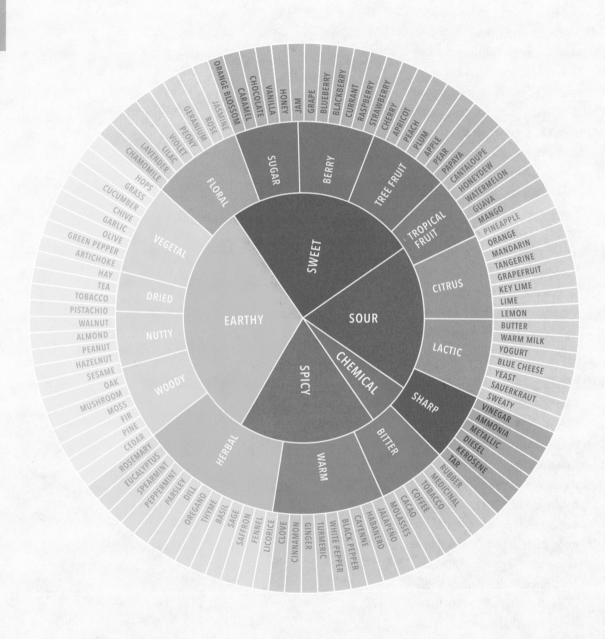

Terpenes

If you're familiar with naturopathic medicine—or if you've spent any time at a high-end-cosmetics counter—you've probably heard the term "essential oils." Those beautiful (and expensive) fragrances that go into your perfume or aromatherapy diffuser are made up of concentrated doses of terpenes, and they contribute not just to cannabis's aroma and flavor, but to its physiological effects as well. In terms of growing, terpenes also play an important role in protecting the plants from bacteria, fungus, and pests.

Terpenes are organic chemical compounds, and there are tens of thousands of them found throughout the plant kingdom. Just over 200 have been identified in cannabis. The terpene ratios of each strain—combined with the various cannabinoids—make up an incredibly complex arrangement; in addition to the effects that each terpene provides on its own, the way they interact with one another and with a strain's particular cannabinoids creates a vast range of outcomes. Again, this is known as the entourage effect, and if you're accustomed to skimming labels solely for THC and CBD content, you should know that your experience with each strain is dictated by much, much more.

Think of each strain's combination of cannabinoids and terpenes as a unique fingerprint. Cannabis researchers have begun cataloging these fingerprints to trace, identify, and verify strains; one day they'll be able to certify that the Platinum Girl Scout Cookies found in a dispensary in Denver is indeed the same authentic strain you tried in Oregon.

Research into the role of terpenes in therapeutic and psychoactive experiences is only relatively recent—benefits are still being uncovered, and not every claim you might find on the internet is definitive. Still, we tend to think that if you're going to the trouble of growing at home, you ought to have a basic knowledge of the key terpene varieties.

PINENE (α & ß)

Pine, fir.

Anti-inflammatory, local antiseptic, expectorant, bronchodilator (potentially helpful for asthmatics), and promotes alertness and memory retention by inhibiting the metabolic breakdown of acetylcholinesterase (a neurotransmitter in the brain that stimulates these cognitive effects). α-Pinene has been used as a cancer-fighting agent in Chinese medicine for many years and is believed to lessen the psychoactive effects of THC.

Oh so many things! α-Pinene is one of the most ubiquitous terpenes in the plant world; it's commonly found in balsamic resin, pine woods, olives, rosemary, sassafras, bergamot, and certain citrus fruits. β-Pinene is found in hops and cumin.

MYRCENE

Musky, earthy, cloves.

Sedative (levels above .5% are thought to produce couch-lock), muscle relaxant, hypnotic, pain reliever, anti-inflammatory, and antimutagenic; also inhibits the action of several known carcinogens. Myrcene is thought to enhance the psychoactive effects of THC by lowering resistance across the blood-to-brain barrier. Basically it allows chemicals (and cannabinoids such as THC) to cross the barrier more quickly. Myrcene also increases the maximum saturation level of your CB1 receptor, which allows for a greater maximum psychoactive effect.

Sweet basil, bay leaves, eucalyptus, wild thyme, lemongrass, ylang-ylang, verbena, and citrus fruits. Myrcene is the most common terpene found in cannabis—you'll probably recognize its flavor and aroma from hops. Ever hear that eating mangoes before you smoke will magnify your high? There's science behind it. Mangoes are loaded with myrcene, and eating one 45 minutes before you smoke may result in a faster onset, and greater intensity, of your high.

LIMONENE

Orange peels.

Mood and attitude improvement, heartburn and gastric acid-reflux relief, combats fungus and antimicrobial pathogenic bacteria, and potentially a chemopreventive agent. Limonene is absorbed through inhalation and quickly appears in your bloodstream, assisting in the absorption of other terpenes as well. It's been found in some studies to promote weight loss. Growing strains high in limonene will help you ward off unwanted insects in your garden.

Oranges, lemons, lime, rosemary, juniper, peppermint, and several pine-needle oils. Frequently used in fragrances, food flavorings, and as a natural renewable solvent in cleaning agents.

LINALOOL

2

AROMA

Fresh, floral, lavender.

BENEFITS

Anxiety and stress reduction, anticonvulsant, antipsychotic, amplifies serotonin-receptor transmission resulting in a euphoric and antidepressant effect. Studies have suggested it boosts immunity and restores cognitive and emotional functions (think: Alzheimer's treatment). Linalool is known to reduce skin scarring when applied topically. It may also reduce lung inflammation for smokers. It's been proven effective as an insecticide, particularly against fruit flies, fleas, and cockroaches. Linalool is crucial for the production of vitamin E in the body.

ALSO FOUND IN

Lavender, mints, laurels, cinnamon, rosewood, birch, palmarosa oil, sweet orange, and some fungi.

ß-CARYOPHYLLENE

AROMA

Spicy and warm, woody, peppery.

BENEFITS

Antioxidant, anti-inflammatory, antinociceptive, gastro-protective, beneficial in ulcer and arthritis treatment, promising as a therapeutic treatment for autoimmune disorders and chronic pain. β-Caryophyllene is the only terpene known to directly activate a cannabinoid receptor, and it's thought of as a "dietary cannabinoid" for its ability to bind to the CB2 receptors found in your gut, spleen, liver, heart, kidneys, bones, blood vessels, lymph cells, endocrine glands, and reproductive organs. Many believe that it also counteracts or lessens the effects of THC.

ALSO FOUND IN

Oregano, Thai basil, cloves, cinnamon leaves, rosemary, and dark, leafy greens (which also activate your CB2 receptors). Ever heard that you should smell fresh-ground black pepper if you ever feel "too high"? There's science behind this one too! Black pepper contains a lot of ß-caryophyllene, and its aroma can help lessen the paranoia you may feel as a result of a little too much THC.

TERPINOLENE
(Γ-TERPINENE)

AROMA

Smoky, woody, citrusy sweetness.

BENEFITS

Antianxiety, insect repellant (particularly mosquitoes and weevils), antifungal, antibacterial, antioxidant, antiseptic, anticancer (reduces the protein expression of AKT1 and K562 cells and inhibits cell proliferation). Terpinolene is a central nervous system depressant and so is often used as a sleep aid.

ALSO FOUND IN

Sage, rosemary, Monterey cypress, lilac, apple, cumin, tea tree.

NEROLIDOL

AROMA

Fresh, woody, floral.

BENEFITS

Sedative, skin penetrant (nerolidol allows cannabinoids to be more easily absorbed by the skin when used topically).

ALSO FOUND IN

Neroli oil, ginger, jasmine.

CAMPHENE

Herbal, fir, damp forest floor.

May be critically important in fighting cardiovascular disease. Studies suggest that it could one day be used as an alternative to damaging pharmaceutical lipid-lowering agents.

Turpentine, camphor oil, citronella oil, ginger oil, and valerian. Camphene is also often used in food flavorings and fragrances.

HUMULENE
(α-CARYOPHYLLENE)

Hops.

Antitumor, antibacterial, analgesic, and, when blended with β-caryophyllene, a powerful anti-inflammatory. Frequently used in Chinese medicine to aid in weight loss due to its appetite-suppressing powers.

Hops (it's what gives beers their "hoppy" flavor), Vietnamese coriander, sage, ginseng.

CARENE

Sweet, citrusy.

While most won't view this as a benefit, carene is an astringent, used to dry out body fluids like tears, mucus, sweat, and excess menstrual flow; as a result it can lead to the "cottonmouth" sensation associated with cannabis. It's also partially responsible for side effects like coughing and dry, red eyes.

Bell peppers, basil, citrus rinds (lemons, limes, mandarins, tangerines, oranges, kumquats), cypress, cedar, juniper, fir, pine. Carene is a major component of turpentine and is often used as a flavoring agent.

GERANIOL

Sweet rose.

Antioxidant, mosquito repellant, and has shown potential as a neuropathy treatment. In one study, geraniol was shown to suppress pancreatic tumor growth.

Roses, geraniums, and often used in retail fragrances.

EUCALYPTOL (CINEOLE)

Menthol, herbaceous.

Antiseptic, antibacterial, antifungal, anti-inflammatory, analgesic, and antioxidant. Eucalyptol is also thought to inhibit cancer-cell growth. It is frequently used topically to increase circulation for pain and to reduce swelling. When its vapor or smoke is inhaled, it can have an uplifting, clarifying effect that results in noticeably increased mental and physical energy.

Eucalyptus, tea tree, bay leaves, mugwort, basil, sage.

PHYTOL

Floral, balsamic.

Immunosuppressant, prevents vitamin A teratogenesis, and when used topically can reduce itching and aid in slow-healing tissue wounds.

Green tea. One of the constituents of chlorophyll, phytol is used by insects to deter predators.

GUAIOL

AROMA

Woody, spicy, vanilla.

BENEFITS

Has been used as a local anesthetic, antiseptic, and an intestinal disinfectant.

ALSO FOUND IN

Artificial vanilla flavorings.

BISABOLOL

AROMA

Tangy, citrus, floral, sweet.

BENEFITS

Antiaging, anti-irritant, anti-inflammatory, antimicrobial, analgesic, antibiotic, and may inhibit cancer-cell growth (it's recently been shown to induce apoptosis in models of leukemia).

ALSO FOUND IN

German chamomile.

P-CYMENE

AROMA

Orange and carrot; when synthesized can have a turpentine-like odor.

BENEFITS

Antimicrobial, antioxidant, and studies suggest it may protect against acute lung injury.

ALSO FOUND IN

Cumin and thyme.

ISOPULEGOL

AROMA

Minty, cooling, bittersweet, medicinal.

BENEFITS

Gastro-protective, anti-inflammatory, and shown to reduce the severity of seizures in animal studies.

ALSO FOUND IN

Cosmetics and chewing gum, where it's used as a flavoring. It's the chemical precursor to menthol.

OCIMENE

AROMA

Tropical, green, woody, vegetal.

BENEFITS

Helpful for gardeners, as it builds up a plant's natural defenses; antifungal.

ALSO FOUND IN

Green mango.

Chapter Three

CONCEPTUALIZING YOUR GARDEN

ALL PROJECTS BENEFIT FROM A LITTLE MORE PLANNING ON THE FRONT END, but it's particularly important for those that require a significant investment of time or financial resources. This chapter is intended to walk you through some of the key components of a grow room so that when it comes time to set up your space, you have a good idea of what's feasible and what's effective. We'd recommend reading the chapter through once, taking a look at our various schematics, then reading the chapter again. Think of it sort of like that old piece of carpenter wisdom: measure twice, cut once.

A home cannabis garden is never a one-size-fits-all affair; it's a mix of what's available to you and how available you are for it. It will be determined by your space, your climate, your budget, and your spare time. You will have to account for temperature, humidity, carbon dioxide, airflow, and light. A good grasp of each of these elements— and how they relate to healthy plants—will go a long way when it comes time to figure out a system that's right for you, your home, and your budget.

In Chapter Four, we'll walk you through the specifics of a few grow room designs, but if you don't have a decent grasp of the basic concepts behind them, you'll have a hard time translating what's on the page to the realities of your home garden. Every one of these categories is a rabbit hole—you can go as deep as your interest takes you—but our goal is to provide as much information as is necessary without overwhelming you.

Open Air vs. Closed Air

There are two categories of home garden: open air and closed air. Both have their advantages and drawbacks, so it's important to think through your needs, preferences, and limitations before committing to one or the other.

An open-air garden, as the name suggests, circulates air between your grow room and the outside world—that might entail a couple of open windows with good screens, or it might mean a system of ducts and a high-grade carbon filter. Either way, you're introducing the plants to naturally occurring carbon dioxide (CO_2) and ensuring that the oxygen they emit has ample opportunity to escape. Open-air gardens may still require amendments—heating and cooling, humidifying and dehumidifying—but your grow room will not be a bubble cut off from the rest of your home or property. In most cases, an open-air garden is easier to get off the ground, cheaper to build, and is less of a blow to your energy bills. These setups do, however, require more frequent adjustments, as they're in tune with the ever-changing conditions of their environment.

A closed-air system requires a combination of air-conditioning, heating, moisture treatment, and carbon dioxide enrichment. In this kind of setup, you never purposely introduce fresh air to the garden. Carbon dioxide is emitted or generated, and the air is constantly recycled. Closed-air systems allow for maximum control, but they take a little more technical know-how from the outset. They can be great for growers with limited time or limited mobility, as they typically require little to no day-to-day tweaking once they're dialed in.

While hybrid systems do exist—most use some kind of secondary buffer space—for the purposes of most home growers and most climates, they're either overly complicated or wasteful.

QUESTIONS TO ASK YOURSELF

HOW MUCH TIME DO YOU HAVE? AND HOW MUCH MONEY ARE YOU WILLING TO SPEND?

Carefully consider your schedule in terms of garden construction; your plants will suffer if you bite off more than you can chew. Forking over a little more money at the outset can save you time, both in terms of building your space and maintaining it.

WHAT DOES YOUR STATE LAW HAVE TO SAY?

Get familiar with local laws and regulations around cannabis cultivation and possession. The number of plants you can legally grow and the amount of cannabis you can legally possess varies, and some states even specify how obscured your plants must be from public view.

WHERE IS THE SPACE LOCATED?

An outbuilding—like a shed or freestanding garage—will have different options and requirements than a fully submerged basement. You'll be making different decisions when it comes to heating, cooling, and airflow.

WHAT SPACE IS AVAILABLE?

How big is your potential garden space? How tall is the ceiling? What's the footprint? Are there windows or other natural options for ventilation? Is it a high-traffic area? As you'll see in the pages that follow, the answers to these questions can make a big difference in your design.

Temperature

Whether you're working with an open-air system or a closed one, maintaining proper temperatures is crucial. For the most part, plants prefer a sweet spot of 75–80°F when the lights are blaring, and 68–75°F when they're not. If it's too hot—above 80°F or so—plants are using their energy to stay cool, instead of using it to grow larger or produce flowers. At 95°F, photosynthesis stops completely. If it's too cool—anywhere below 60°F—the plant's metabolism slows down, as does photosynthesis. If temperatures drop to 40°F, you risk tissue damage.

Ideal temperatures depend on a few factors. Each strain is slightly different—this often comes down to its climate of origin—and you should consult whomever you're buying genetics from about best practices. (Most seed and clone banks make this information available.) Carbon dioxide levels affect the optimal temperature range as well; if you're supplementing CO_2 and operating above 400 parts per million (ppm), you'll want to increase the heat a bit. But generally, the change in temperature will be governed by where your plants are in the grow cycle.

While there may not be a wide range in the *ideal* temperatures, achieving them in the reality of your garden will probably be trickier than you'd think—there's a wide range of contributing factors. If you're using an open-air system, you have to consider that external conditions will be different in an attic than they will be in a basement, and different in a hallway closet than they will be in a storage shed. (They'll also vary from season to season.) You'll need to factor in other equipment—heat-producing lights are the biggest culprit, but you should account for ballasts and fan motors as well. In the winter, this equipment might keep your garden right where it needs to be—and make a space heater unnecessary—but in the summer, it can quickly get too hot. If this is the case, it's best to establish your light cycle during the night, when temperatures are cooler, and your dark cycle during the day, to prevent overheating. Still, there's a good chance you'll want to invest in an air conditioner as well. (Wait until you've set up your lights and fan to purchase one, so you have a good idea of what, if anything, you'll need.)

The most important place to measure heat is directly under the lights—usually the warmest part of the room—and at the surface of your canopy, where new growth is occurring. A good temperature gauge is important; we recommend an infrared kitchen thermometer, which will help you take precise readings of particular locations.

TEMPERATURE CHEAT SHEET

Germination:	75°F
Vegetative Growth:	75°F
Flowering Growth (Day Cycle):	77°F
Flowering Growth (Night Cycle):	68°F

Humidity

Finding the right humidity for your garden is something of a balancing act: Too much, you risk exposing your plants to mold and rot; you also discourage the rate of transpiration (see page 110), which can stunt your plants. But not enough and you risk drying out the foliage, which likewise discourages growth. As with temperature, the optimal relative humidity varies based on where your plants are in their grow cycle. (Relative humidity, if you're in need of a refresher, is the ratio of water vapor in the air as a percentage of the saturation point at a given temperature.) During germination and the first few days of vegetative growth, you want your relative humidity to be around 80%. For the rest of vegetation, it should be 70–75%. Over the course of flowering, you will gradually want to get the relative humidity down to 40%. (We'll walk you through ideal week-by-week levels in Chapter Seven.)

If your garden happens to be too dry—as sometimes happens in open-air systems during the summer—it's fairly easy to add moisture. Oftentimes, it's enough to throw a pitcher's worth of water on the ground and let it evaporate. You can set up a misting system—similar to what you'd see in a grocery store produce department—or you can, from time to time, take your garden hose and mist the plants. At more extreme levels, you might use a small humidifier during vegetative growth. All of this should be done under the heat of your lights; this helps the water evaporate into the air.

The more common problem, however, is too much humidity. Because your plants are constantly pulling water through their roots and transpiring through their leaves, they're continually adding moisture to the air. In an open-air system, natural ventilation, such as an open window or an exhaust duct—aided by a decent fan—will usually be enough. If you end up needing to use an air conditioner, it too will pull moisture from the air and lower your humidity levels. If you're growing in a closed-air system, you'll almost certainly need to invest in a dehumidifier. (They're relatively inexpensive, and allow you to get your humidity right where you want it—just be sure to empty the water reservoir daily to avoid mold.)

HUMIDITY CHEAT SHEET

Germination: 80%
Vegetative Growth: 70–75%
Flowering Growth (Day Cycle): 40–65%

Carbon Dioxide

If you remember your photosynthesis unit from high school biology (for a refresher, see page 110), you know that, along with light, plants need water and carbon dioxide to create energy. Plants absorb CO_2 through their stomata—the pore-like holes on the underside of their leaves—and then it is converted into sugars. The concentration of CO_2 in the earth's atmosphere ranges between 390–400 parts per million (though any reputable climate scientist will warn you that that number is on the rise), which is adequate for cannabis. Still, the more CO_2 your plants absorb—to a point, and depending on how much light is available—the more mass your plants can create. This means faster growth and more robust plants—leaves are thicker and more turgid, stems are stronger.

If you're using an open-air system, the natural levels of CO_2 will suffice. If you have proper air intake—and a good fan to help it along—you'll be fine. If you're using a closed-air system (or if you want to supplement what's already there in your open-air garden), you'll need to provide it. In a small enclosed space, it will take only a few hours for a full-sized plant to suck up all the available CO_2. If the levels drop to about 200 ppm, photosynthesis will effectively stop and, gradually, the plant's essential functions will shut down.

Advocates of CO_2 enrichment have found that the ideal level for cannabis growth is in the neighborhood of 1,200 ppm, but keep in mind that your lights need to be strong enough to power all that photosynthesis. Higher levels of CO_2 also require slightly higher temperatures. While a normal 400 ppm garden might do best at 75°F—depending on strain and where you are in the grow cycle—an enriched garden will do better at 82°F.

The easiest and most effective way to introduce CO_2 is with a tank and an emitter system (these are discussed in more detail in Chapter Four). The levels are regulated, the CO_2 is added only while the lights are on, and there are no tricky side effects, like excess heat. Still, other growers have been known to use generators—which burn gas or propane—dry ice, compost piles, and fermented liquids to give their plants a CO_2 boost. (We can't—or won't—recommend these methods, either because they're ineffective, inefficient, or dangerous.)

Airflow

CIRCULATION

We've established that cannabis is greedy for carbon dioxide—it takes only minutes for leaves to absorb all the CO_2 molecules in their vicinity. And since those leaves are simultaneously emitting oxygen and water, they're creating dead space that does nothing for photosynthesis. It's your job, then, to make sure that new air is constantly circulating around and through your garden, renewing CO_2 levels and allowing plants to execute their essential functions. Maintaining proper airflow is likewise important for temperature and humidity issues, since moist, stagnant air is an invitation to mold and disease.

In an open-air system, you're bringing fresh air in and moving stale air out; you need proper ventilation and exhaust. In some setups, an open window is enough (just make sure you have adequate screens to keep pests out). In others, it means a system of ductwork and a powerful in-line fan. Since hot air rises, it's best if your ventilation is below the canopy line and your exhaust above it on the opposite side of the room; this creates a natural flow of air through your plants. It's important to encourage air to circulate *within* the grow room as well. This is accomplished easily enough with strategically placed fans. By creating a breeze, you move hot, dead air out from under the canopy and let fresh air take its place.

In a closed-air system, the same principles apply, but it's even more critical that you keep air from stagnating; the stakes are simply higher. If you end up with, say, an incursion of powdery mildew, it will only be fostered by the recycled air. The key to proper circulation in a closed environment is the position of your various pieces of equipment—particularly the air conditioner, dehumidifier, and fans—in relation to the plants and in relation to each other. You don't want the A/C blowing directly on one side of the garden and the heat from the dehumidifier's exhaust blowing directly on the other. Your strategically placed fans can create horizontal airflow that will blend the varying temperatures before air hits the plants. In order to get the moisture levels correct, the dehumidifier should be pulling in a representative sample of the air from the room; since the intake is usually on one side and exhaust on the other, be sure the unit is positioned in such a way that it's not primarily pulling in its own dry, treated air.

AIR FILTERS AND ODOR

In an open-air system, filters aren't *necessarily* needed. Careful attention to your plants and screens on your windows will usually be enough. But if you live in a particularly polluted or dusty location—by the freeway or near a chemical plant—a simple air filter, the kind of product you'd use in your home's heating or cooling system, might be advisable. The problem with air filters on your intake, beyond the added expense, is that while they restrict undesirable particles, they also restrict airflow—by as much as 50%. This means your fans will need to do twice as much work.

In closed-air systems, where the air is recycled and the stakes of decontamination are higher, you may want to invest in a carbon filter. While in-line models can be attached to the ductwork of an open-air grow room's exhaust, in closed systems, you'll need to opt for a stand-alone unit. In either case, a fan draws the air through the filter, which—through a chemical process called adsorption—causes atoms to adhere to the activated carbon. By the time the air comes out the other side, it's good as new.

Carbon filters are especially useful when it comes to dealing with odor. It should come as no surprise that cannabis is a pungent plant. While we quite like its aroma, we can't blame you if you're concerned that it will overwhelm the places you eat, sleep, and live. Depending on your space and setup, it's possible that decent ventilation will be enough. But some spaces, and some living situations, need a more substantial solution. For a larger garden, a carbon filter is your best option. It can scrub the air so thoroughly that your neighbors won't know what you're up to in that garage. (This is helpful whether you're dealing with squares *or* mooches.) In an open-air garden, an in-line filter connected to your exhaust system is the most thorough and efficient setup. But if you just want to mitigate the odor—to keep a tented garden in the basement from overpowering the whole house—you might opt for the kind of stand-alone unit described above.

NOISE

Fans can be noisy—particularly the kind needed in larger grow rooms. The simplest option is just to grow in a location where the sound won't bother you. But if your space is limited and the noise drives you nuts, it might be worth investing in (or DIYing) an isolation cabinet that will muffle or mute the noise. You don't need to be a physics major to understand that when too much air is forced through too small an opening, the noise can be unpleasant. (Ask the nearest grade schooler or hack comedian to explain this concept.) If you're using ductwork for your exhaust, it's important that the opening is size-appropriate for the amount of air you want to move. If you're hearing a constant whooshing sound, you might need a bigger duct.

Light

Light plays two essential roles in cannabis cultivation: it provides energy by way of photosynthesis (see page 110), and, through its on-and-off cycles, communicates to the plant when to use its energy on vegetative growth and when to begin flowering.

From there, as you might imagine, things become a bit more complicated. While all indoor setups, on some level, aim to replicate and exaggerate the qualities of the light that cannabis would absorb in the wild, it's important to remember that the sun is a full-spectrum light source, and huge portions of that spectrum do little or nothing for your plants. The sun doesn't have to worry about energy bills, but you probably should.

There are numerous types of lamps and numerous ways to use them. Each has advantages, disadvantages, and strategies. When deciding what lights are right for your garden, there are three main considerations to take into account: up-front cost, efficiency, and efficacy. The first is pretty straightforward, and can be determined by browsing a few catalogs online and checking out price tags. While short-term cost is always a consideration, if you're growing at any kind of scale or for any amount of time, it's worth thinking about long-term costs and the difference that each lamp can make for your plants. But before we delve any deeper or begin to analyze the options, there are a few concepts worth exploring.

THE LIGHT SPECTRUM

When you consider the entire spectrum of electromagnetic radiation, the portion of light that is visible to the human eye is relatively narrow. There are wavelengths and frequencies beyond what we can process that, nonetheless, are crucial for cannabis growth. And for the purpose of that growth, not all light is equal; different wavelengths are critical at different periods in the plant's life cycle.

The angle of the sun and the way that light passes through the atmosphere determines what part of the spectrum we experience. During the long days of late spring and early summer, the sun's rays are entering the atmosphere at something like a 90° angle; as a result, we get more blue light. As the earth tilts, the days grow shorter, and summer turns to fall, more of our light is on the red end of the spectrum. Plants use blue light in the germination of seeds and seedlings and in the development of stems, leaves, and stalks. (This is the period we call vegetative growth.) When it comes time to produce flowers, plants primarily use red light. You've probably noticed this pattern in the foliage around you as the seasons change. We should also note that different wavelengths are tied to the maximum absorption of different chemicals in plants (including chlorophyll and beta-carotene, importantly).

LIGHT SPECTRUM AND PLANT ABSORPTION

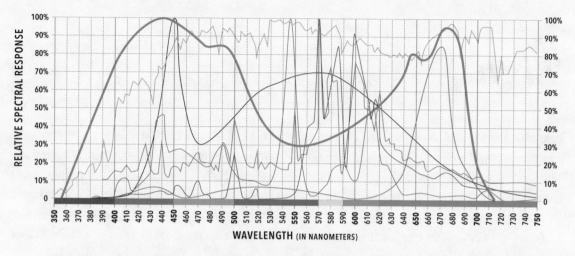

NOTE: *Because intensity can be adjusted based on a fixture's wattage, or even by adding more lights, this graph won't tell you much in terms of sheer amount of usable light. Each curve is scaled for the sake of comparison. What we aim to demonstrate is where each type of light peaks throughout the spectrum. Importantly, peaks in areas outside of the Plant Response Curve indicate wasted energy.*

PLANT RESPONSE (——):
This curve represents a plant's maximum light absorption at different points on the spectrum. In a perfect world, a light source would follow this curve precisely and no energy would be wasted creating unusable light.

SPECTRUM OF SUNLIGHT (——):
This curve represents the sun's light spectrum at high noon. Notice how much unusable light the sun creates relative to what a plant needs to grow.

SPECTRUM OF A TYPICAL HPS LAMP(——):
Most of an HPS lamp's energy is used to produce light in the 550–610 nm range. The green/yellow/orange range of the spectrum is the lowest part of the Plant Response Curve and thus the least efficient area in terms of light production.

SPECTRUM OF A TYPICAL MH LAMP(——):
The MH lamp produces a similar peak to the HPS lamp in the 600 nm range but has a higher relative peak in the blue end of the spectrum. While there is still a lot of wasted energy, this blue light is great for vegetative growth and for certain parts of the flowering process.

FLUORESCENT T5 LAMP(——):
Agricultural fluorescent lamps come in a range of spectrums. The one shown here is geared toward blue light, but still has significant output in the yellow spectrum. While fluorescents tend to be far more efficient than HPS bulbs, they still spend a lot of energy on light that plants can't use.

SPECTRUM OF A TYPICAL VEGETATIVE LED** (——):
LEDs made for vegetative growth produce most of their light in the 430–450 nm range. They peak right in the middle of the blue range, which is perfect for vegetative growth. Many lamps will produce some light in the green/yellow range, above the Plant Response Curve, but unlike HPS and MH lamps, it's a shallower secondary curve.

SPECTRUM OF A TYPICAL FLOWERING LED**(——):
LEDs made for flowering growth produce most of their light in the 650–680 nm range. Their peaks closely mimic the Plant Response Curve's movement in the red end of the spectrum. Flowering LEDs typically provide a small amount of light in the blue range of the spectrum, which supports continued vegetative growth, but the vast majority of the energy goes toward red light.

*** LED lights are incredibly varied. Our samples are based on high-quality grow lights made for agricultural use. The LED market has become flooded with shoddy, poorly designed products, and we encourage you to seek out reputable manufacturers.*

MEASURING LIGHT

When it comes to measuring light, there are two commonly used terms you'll quickly come across: lumens and PAR. Lumens (lm) measure the intensity of light visible to the human eye. (Lumens are for humans, as they say.) As we've established, plants use wavelengths far beyond what the human eye can take in. Thus, this particular unit doesn't have much meaning to your plants. When it comes to growing, any advice or rule of thumb that uses lumens can quickly be discarded (you'd be surprised how often this comes up).

What you *should* care about is PAR, or Photosynthetically Active Radiation. This is the spectrum of light—spanning 400 to 700 nanometers (nm)—that plants can use for growth. PAR is discussed in terms of a unit called micromoles (μmol). These can be measured with a meter, but such devices are quite expensive and probably not a priority for most home growers. (If a light manufacturer doesn't mention PAR, there's probably a reason they aren't disclosing the details; we suggest you find yourself another light.)

When deciding what kind of light to use, there are a few terms and measurements you'll need to be familiar with. We've divided them into two broad categories: Intensity and Efficiency. Intensity addresses the quality of the light in terms of its ability to provide energy to the plant. Efficiency is a way to measure how much energy it took to produce that usable light. You must address both categories in order to determine what light is best for you and your garden.

INTENSITY

PPF (Photosynthetic Photon Flux) measures the total light output in terms of micromoles of photons produced per second ($\mu mol/s$).

PPFD (Photosynthetic Photon Flux Density) measures the number of micromoles of photons striking a square meter per second ($\mu mol/m^2/s$). While this measurement is more directly applicable to growers, be warned: manufacturers sometime juke the stats by measuring closer to the lights than would be ideal for most plants. (This is why, when comparing lights, the raw PPF number is also valuable.)

EFFICIENCY

WATTAGE, in this context, refers to the amount of energy used to power a light bulb (W = amp x volt).

JOULE (J) is the unit of measurement for the energy it takes to produce 1 watt of power for 1 second.

MICROMOLES PER JOULE is the most useful rubric for the efficiency of your grow lights. It measures the number of micromoles of photons produced by every joule of electrical energy ($\mu mol/J$).

So, let's say a light produces 1,000 $\mu mol/s$ and uses 500 watts to produce it. That's a PAR efficacy of 2.0 $\mu mol/J$. Now, if that light covers 20 square feet, you know that each square foot of light requires 0.1 $\mu mol/J$. If you run this formula for various fixtures, you can quickly compare how much energy each light uses to do the same amount of work.

METAL HALIDE (MH)

Vegetative growth.

Peaks in the 400–600 nm range (with very little above 600 nm).

Units usually consist of a 250- to 1,000-watt bulb, a reflector, and a cord that connects to an external ballast. These fixtures are lightweight, and an attached chain makes them easy to hang.

Fairly inexpensive to get started. Their durability combined with the fact that it's an older technology means you can often find fixtures on the used market (although you'll probably want to spring for new bulbs). You can use a single fixture with metal halide bulbs for vegetative growth and high-pressure sodium bulbs for flowering.

Not as efficient as other options; much of the energy is used creating light outside the plant's ideal spectrum. Creates more excess heat than LED lights.

HIGH-PRESSURE SODIUM (HPS)

Flowering growth.

Peaks in the 500–700 nm range.

Units usually consist of a 150- to 1,000-watt bulb, a reflector, and a cord that connects to an external ballast. These fixtures are lightweight, and an attached chain makes them easy to hang.

Good spectrum for flowering growth. Since they tend to be mass-produced, the up-front cost is low. You can use a single fixture with metal halide bulbs for vegetative growth and high pressure sodium bulbs for flowering.

Very hot and inefficient. Less than 15% of the light is emitted as PAR, so much of the energy is wasted on parts of the spectrum plants can't use. Bulbs typically need to be replaced annually.

CERAMIC METAL HALIDE

Supplemental light, particularly during flowering growth.

Full spectrum with peaks throughout the usable range. Additionally, ceramic bulbs emit UV-B rays, which—studies suggest—encourage increased resin production during flowering (researchers believe that resin is part of the plant's natural defense against harmful radiation from the sun). On a related note, if you're exposing *yourself* to this light, use protective eyewear and apply sunscreen.

While you could, theoretically, use ceramic bulbs from start to finish, they're more effective as a companion to other lights. Since metal halide (MH) and high-pressure sodium (HPS) bulbs can be used in the same fixtures, you could—in a 4-light set-up—use 2 MH bulbs and 2 ceramic during vegetative growth, and swap out the MH for HPS during flowering. (Be sure to set them up in a checkerboard pattern to take advantage of their respective benefits.) Not all ballasts are suitable for ceramic bulbs; make sure to check the label before using.

Ceramic lamps use significantly less energy per usable micromole than MH or HPS bulbs. UV-B rays are thought to increase resin production and thus the potency of cannabis.

Steep price tag, and bulbs must be replaced periodically. Their light spectrum is not quite as well-suited for vegetative growth as MH, nor as ideal for flowering as HPS. These are not the most widely used lights on the market, so it might be harder to troubleshoot when issues come up.

FLUORESCENT

IDEAL USE

Vegetative and flowering growth. Also great for developing young clones.

SPECTRUM COVERED

400–500 nm during vegetative growth; 500–700 nm during flowering.

SETUP

Standard fluorescent lights come in tubes with diameters ranging from 5/8" to 1½". (The former, classified as "T-5," are the most efficient.) They require a special fixture, which should be used in combination with a ballast and a reflector hood. Compact fluorescents make for an even simpler setup, as they fit in standard light sockets, but since they don't have much throw or intensity, you'll need to keep your garden—and your individual plants—relatively small.

ADVANTAGES

Minimal initial investment, and bulbs tend to be long-lasting. There are a variety of available spectrums among fluorescent bulbs, which can be taken advantage of during different phases of the grow cycle. Bulbs labeled "cool white" emit more blue light, making them ideal for vegetative growth, while those labeled "warm white" emit more red light, which encourages flowering.

DISADVANTAGES

Inefficient compared to LEDs—and T-5s are much hotter. Very little throw (the ability for light to penetrate into a canopy) and less intensity than high-pressure sodium lights.

LED (LIGHT-EMITTING DIODES)

IDEAL USE

Vegetative and flowering growth.

SPECTRUM COVERED

Since diodes can be tailored to specific outputs, LED lights can cover nearly all spectrums.

SETUP

Varies based on the individual system, but since they're designed for indoor growing, LED fixtures typically come with all the necessary equipment built in (along with installation and operating instructions).

ADVANTAGES

As the fixtures are created specifically for plants' various phases of growth, there's almost no energy wasted on light outside the usable spectrum. LED is an all-around more efficient technology, with long-lasting fixtures and no bulbs to replace. Fixtures are relatively compact and give off very little heat, which makes them suitable for tight spaces.

DISADVANTAGES

New technology is expensive. When individual diodes start to go out—usually about ten years in with regular use—the fixture will no longer be effective. Not quite as good a throw as HPS, so you need to keep the fixture a little closer to the plant. Due to the intensity of the red spectrum, the light can cause slight bleaching at the plant's tips, which makes chlorophyll synthesis more difficult. Generally, fixtures are phase-specific—one for vegetative growth, one for flowering—which is not ideal for a single-room setup as you'd have to swap the fixture out between growth phases for ideal conditions.

Chapter Four

SETTING UP YOUR GROW ROOM

CHAPTER THREE LAID THE FOUNDATION—HELPED YOU ENVISION A CANNABIS garden based on your available space, your lifestyle, and the fundamental needs of the plants. This chapter moves from principle toward practice and introduces a series of indoor garden designs that we can happily vouch for. We settled on these particular plans for three main reasons: they're easily tailored to a variety of spaces; the needed equipment is both easy to find and easy to operate; and with the right amount of diligence, they tend to produce a successful yield of crops.

These gardens are divided into two categories: closed air and open air. The former is air-conditioned, temperature controlled, and sealed off from the rest of your home. As such, it ends up being a little more expensive, in terms of both equipment and energy bills. The latter exchanges the air in the garden with the air in the rest of your home or the air outdoors. It tends to come with a smaller price tag, but means a little less control of the environment.

Many serious growers opt for two separate grow rooms: one space is used for vegetative growth—along with mother plants and clones—while the other is used for flowering, which requires different levels of humidity and different hours of light. If you have the space and resources, you can always upgrade to a two-room setup, but if you're just beginning, our advice is to start small and simple.

While our models are fairly specific, they're also scalable. We encourage you to take these designs and tailor them to fit your needs—expand, contract, reconfigure, decorate, etc. But before we get into the plans themselves, let's walk through the equipment you'll be working with.

Equipment

Every garden will call for slightly different equipment—a mix of lights and meters, fans and humidifiers—and we'll outline your shopping list directly on the schematic page. But the fundamentals are the same, so first we'd like to spend some time breaking down the equipment itself, detailing what it is you'll be loading into your shopping cart. Whether you're putting together a grow room from scratch or supplementing a prefab kit, we suggest checking out local cannabis, gardening, and hardware stores—along with online retailers—and finding an option that works for you. We always encourage you to support local businesses, but acknowledge that that isn't an option everywhere.

If the space you've chosen for your grow room isn't already wired and ready, take heed: Electrical work should be handled only by licensed professionals. Errors may result in destruction of property, injury, or death. Consider this your warning.

AIRFLOW

In many open-air gardens, you'll need an assist when it comes to bringing in fresh oxygen. We recommend connecting simple 4- to 6-inch in-line fans to your exhaust. In a perfect world, you'd replace all of the air in your grow room roughly 2 times per minute (some growers, in some climates, cycle the air as little as once every 5 minutes, but in our experience such conditions lead to much slower growth). These fans are rated by cubic feet per minute (CPM).

If you have a 5' x 5' x 8' garden, that comes out to 200 cubic feet. In order to cycle the air twice per minute, you'll want something rated at least 400 CFM. (Keep in mind, it's a safe bet to assume that your fan will operate at only about 70–80% of its rating. CFM tests typically take place in controlled environments; real life is rarely so perfect.)

In-line fans come in all shapes and sizes, but whatever type or brand you use, we highly recommend a temperature-based controller that will adjust the fan speed automatically when the room gets too hot or too cool.

Whether you're using an open-air or closed-air setup, you'll also need to facilitate airflow within the grow room. We'll address specific strategies in the schematics themselves, but depending on your setup, you can use wall-mounted, drum, or pedestal fans for this purpose. No need for anything industrial-strength; the goal is to emulate a light breeze, not a windstorm.

AIR CONDITIONING

If you ultimately opt for a closed-air garden, your air-conditioning system will be your workhorse. If you're growing with 1 or 2 lights, 8,000 Btus is a safe bet (Btu = British thermal unit; 1 Btu is equal to the amount of energy used to raise the temperature of 1 lb. of water by 1 degree Fahrenheit). For a 4-light setup, you'll likely want

15,000 Btus. The heat gain from a light, ballast, and fan motor alone typically necessitates 3,500 Btus of cooling, so if you're working with an especially large room, you might consider scaling up.

While a window-mounted or -vented unit will be fine if you just need help cooling down an open-air garden, a closed-air setup will require a ductless split system. The air-handling unit is mounted on the wall of your grow room and connected by refrigerant lines to an external condenser. Since these units don't need to exhaust hot air from the room, they allow you to maintain a truly closed system. These units are highly efficient, but the up-front cost is something to consider—they start around $650 and can run as high as a few thousand.

CO$_2$

Adding CO$_2$ is a requirement in all closed-air gardens, but even in open-air systems, growers will often supplement the amount of carbon dioxide in the room to speed up development, pushing the typical 400 ppm to around 1,200 ppm (see page 60 for more details). The most common method among home growers is a simple emitter system, consisting of a 20- to 50-lb. tank (these can be rented or exchanged—try companies that specialize in beverage supplies or fire extinguishers), a flow meter, a pressure regulator, and a solenoid valve to turn the gas flow on and off. Again, these setups are sold as kits in hydroponic supply outlets, but it's easy enough to pick up what you need at most hardware stores. If you're springing for this kind of system, we suggest splurging on a controller that measures the amount of CO$_2$ in the air and automatically maintains your desired levels.

Some people opt for a CO$_2$ generator, which burns propane or natural gas, thus releasing CO$_2$ into the air.

This is a simple, inexpensive option, but really more appropriate for professional agriculture settings—it's not necessarily safe in a home garden. If your grow room falls into the former camp, do keep in mind that generators produce heat and moisture, both of which are a factor in controlled environments.

HUMIDITY

Your specific needs will depend on moisture levels and the size of your garden—in some setups and climates, natural ventilation will suffice. In an open-air garden, keep an eye on your moisture levels and only spring for another piece of equipment only once you know what you need. But since virtually all of the water you give your plants is eventually transpired, without a dehumidifier, a closed-air garden would quickly turn into a humid swamp. In a single-light setup, you can expect to give your plants 10 gallons of water a day at their neediest. So a small, portable dehumidifier—something with an 80-pint capacity—should do the trick. In a larger garden—something like our 4-light setup—your plants may require roughly 250–300 pints of dehumidification per day at their peak. At that level, you'll need something commercial-grade.

If you're in a particularly dry environment and your humidistat consistently comes in at 40% or lower, you might invest in a small 30-pint humidifier.

GAUGES

Fine-tuning the temperature and humidity in your garden is a must, and it largely depends on the tools that you have to monitor them. Fan controllers often lack a visual temperature readout, but even when they come equipped with such features, we still find it useful to have an analog thermostat for backup. (You might be tempted by the $10 options, but we highly recommend springing for one in the $25–$50 range—that small jump in price translates to a huge jump in quality.) The kind of humidistats used in cigar humidors tend to be both accurate and relatively cheap (not to mention attractive).

For the techies among us, there are now digital interfaces that link your smartphone to temperature, humidity, and CO_2-concentration sensors. Such systems are a great way to keep track of these levels, even when you can't be physically present in your garden. (Though we recommend checking such a system against analog tools from time to time.)

LIGHTS

We broke down your various lighting options in Chapter Three, but if you can stomach the up-front costs, we recommend investing in LED lights. They have many benefits: lower heat gain, lower electrical consumption, fewer hot spots, and, potentially, a better spectrum of light. (You might also check with your local power utility about energy credits.)

The general rule of thumb is that you'll need one 600- to 1000-watt fixture for every 15–25 square feet of growing space. If you settle on one of our smaller garden designs, one light will probably suffice; if you go with one of the larger setups, you're likely looking at four. Remember: you're aiming for 600 micromoles during the vegetative stage, and 1,000 micromoles during flowering.

We think it's wise—especially in a closed-air garden—to connect your fixtures to a temperature controller. This way, if the lights get too hot, they'll automatically shut down rather than scorching your plants.

WATER

We believe in the good old-fashioned watering can—when you take the time to hand-water your garden, you'll grow attuned to your plants' needs (and you'll be able to keep an eye on molds, pests, etc.).

With a larger garden, you may consider a water barrel with a hose attachment and a watering wand. We recommend using a barrel system, rather than connecting directly to your faucet. This allows you to acclimate the water to room temperature, mix in any nutrients, and—by adding a pump to the reservoir—recirculate the water to keep oxygen levels up. Just be sure to position the barrel higher than the top of your pots so that gravity can do its work.

That said, if time is precious and you need to streamline your daily tasks, it's easy enough to cobble together an irrigation system. In addition to your water barrel, this will require a submersible pump, a half-inch polyethylene hose, a coil of quarter-inch spaghetti hose—which you'll connect to the main line with barbed irrigation fittings (for just a couple of dollars, you can purchase a special hole punch that will ensure a proper fit)—and enough drip emitters or sprinkler attachments to satiate those thirsty plants. Be sure to pick up a good compression end-cap for your main line, or you may end up with a flooded basement. To fully automate the process, you can connect your pump to an automatic timer—just be sure to test it with your drip emitters and sprinklers to be certain your plants are getting enough water.

PLANTERS

We love the natural fiber planter bags produced by Root Pouch. They're porous and breathable—a boon for root systems and overall plant health—and they have handles on the side, which makes them easy to move around. If you'd rather go to the local nursery and grab something readily available, a hard plastic 12-inch pot works great as well. Either way, you'll want one receptacle for each of your seeds/clones—don't try to double up—and, of course, the larger the pot, the larger the root system, and the larger the eventual plant. Go with the largest pots that you can get away with in your garden layout. They'll give you a larger buffer for water, more opportunity for root growth, room for companion plants, and—if you're reusing your soil and feeding the microbiome—there'll be more room for that activity as well.

INTERIOR

Since light is the key to steady growing, reflective surfaces are your friends. Depending on what kind of walls you're dealing with, this typically means white paint or reflective sheeting. In growing circles, there is some debate about the best type of paint finish: glossy paints reflect more light—and are easier to clean—but can create hot spots; flat and eggshell finishes aren't quite as reflective and are more prone to mildew, but tend to reflect light more evenly. We're willing to take our chances with the former, as we think the benefits outweigh the risks. But whichever school you find yourself in, be sure to clean the walls thoroughly and apply either a primer or 2 coats of paint (especially if the walls were previously a darker color). The rule of thumb is that you get 400 square feet of coverage per gallon of paint, so plan accordingly.

Of course, if your space doesn't easily lend itself to a thorough new paint job, Mylar, Foylon, or Panda Film will do the trick. Avoid air bubbles and wrinkles where you can—the flatter the better—and be sure that it's securely fastened; once air starts moving through your grow room, any unsecured sheeting will be quick to flutter. On this front, we suggest using double-sided foam tape around the edges, then using a staple gun to apply staples directly through the tape (this method helps to avoid tearing).

Last but not least, the ideal flooring would be water resistant and similarly reflective, but at a minimum, avoid carpets, rugs, or any other especially porous material. Heat and moisture have a way of turning such things into havens for mold and mildew.

GROW TENTS

Not everyone is at liberty to fully transform their basement or attic into a grow room: some of us have square in-laws, unadventurous husbands, or (totally reasonable) landlords. If you find yourself in any such camp, or just want to start small, a prefab grow tent might do the trick. These setups are increasingly easy to find, come in all shapes and sizes, and start at about $70—though certain models will set you back a couple grand. Most come equipped with waterproof bases (so you don't damage your floor), reflective walls, outer overlapping tent seams so that no light escapes, and easy access windows that you can use to monitor your plants without affecting temperature and humidity. They have holes and ports for cords and exhaust, and hangers (and a strong enough frame) to secure your lights. If you decide a grow tent is right for you, see our Open-Air, Single-Light design for additional pointers and principles.

OPEN AIR, SINGLE LIGHT

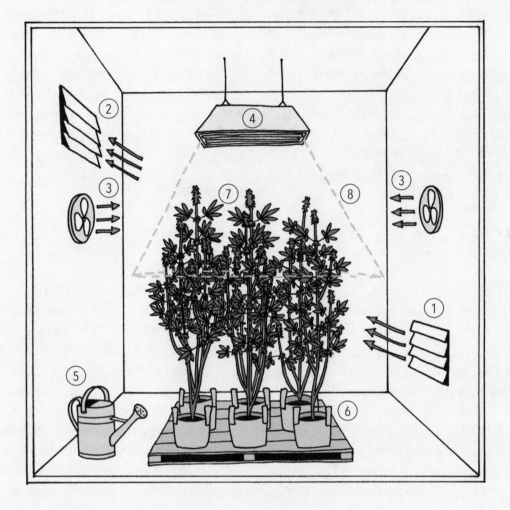

PROs

- Simple, inexpensive way to get started
- Applicable to various small spaces (tents, closets, cabinets, boxes)
- Energy efficient
- Easy to break down
- Fresh air encourages a healthy microbiome

CONs

- Limited canopy space
- Requires a willingness to adjust for temperature and humidity
- Possible exposure to pests from the outdoors
- Potential for heavy cannabis odors

INTAKE (1) / EXHAUST (2)

In an open-air setup, the intake and exhaust will largely govern your airflow. Ideally, the intake will be positioned low and the exhaust up high; the fresh, cool, CO_2-rich air from outside the garden will—as the temperature rises—be pulled though the canopy and make its way to the exhaust. Be sure to keep an eye on the outside air temperature. If you're bringing in air directly from the outdoors, and it's below 60°F, you'll want to make sure that air has a chance to warm up before coming into contact with the plants. A small heater and an upward-facing fan will work wonders.

HORIZONTAL AIR FLOW (3)

In order to prevent temperature variation—along with pockets of dead air where mold and fungi thrive—and to encourage transpiration (see page 110), you need a steady breeze moving throughout your garden. Avoid blowing air directly on to your plants; the idea is to create a gentle, even current through the canopy. In addition to protecting your plants' health, the slight movement from the air encourages strong stalk development during vegetation and more robust growth during flowering.

LIGHT (4)

Whatever light you choose, your fixture should be hung in such a way that it can be easily adjusted up and down. (This can be as simple as using links on a chain or a rope ratchet.) The intensity of light falls off exponentially the farther you get away from it, so maintaining proper distance is crucial to growth and will ensure you get the most bang for your buck. You'll also be grateful for some extra head room when it comes time to inspect, water, train, and trim your plants.

WATER (5)

In the single-light setup, a watering can is probably sufficient. Just be sure that the spout is long enough to reach your pots without bludgeoning your canopy.

POT PLACEMENT (6)

Don't place your pots directly on the floor. A table, a wooden pallet, or some kind of air gap/insulation will allow your pots to maintain room temperature without losing heat to the floor. (If you have insulated floors, this is less of an issue, but elevating your pots will make cleaning and dealing with run-off more convenient.)

PLANT SPACING (7) AND LIGHT FOOTPRINT (8)

Because ideal spacing is particular to your lamp, there's no hard and fast rule. But the principle remains the same: fill the maximum amount of your light footprint with canopy. Even in a tight space, we favor multiple small plants to a single large one; it's easier to keep the canopy evenly lit, and it means less time in vegetative growth. With a single light, we've found that 6–9 plants is ideal. (This assumes 2 to 6 weeks of vegetation, and should produce a full canopy by week 4 of flowering.) Of course, adjusting for different strains, growth rates, and your environment will be an ongoing project.

SHOPPING LIST:

- **LIGHTS:** 600–1,000 W fixture, with timer

- **AIR:** 4"–6" inline exhaust fan with 400 CFM rating (and temperature-based controller); two small horizontal air flow fans

- **GAUGES:** Thermostat and humidistat

- **WATER:** Watering can

- **PLANTERS:** One 5–7 gallon pot for each of your seeds/ clones

- **INTERIOR:** White paint or sheets of Foylon/Mylar; a pallet, table, or something to keep your pots off the ground

CLOSED AIR, SINGLE LIGHT

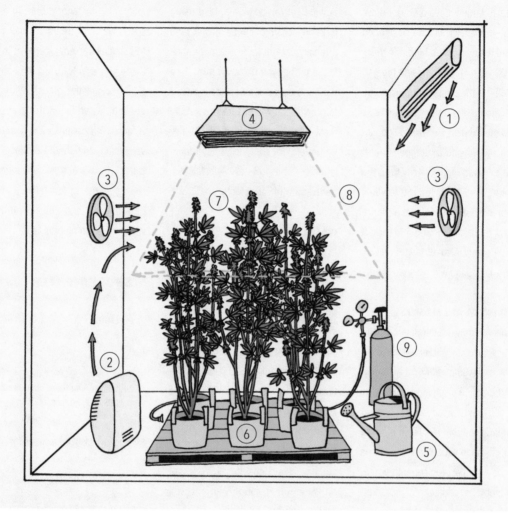

PROs

- Maximum return from a small space

- Low-profile, particularly in terms of odor

- Applicable to various small spaces (tents, closets, cabinets, boxes)

- Once you're set up, fewer adjustments are necessary

CONs

- Limited canopy space

- Uses more energy than an open-air garden

- Higher up-front costs

- If a piece of equipment fails, plants can dramatically suffer or die

AIR CONDITIONER (1)

In a closed-air garden, all of your cooling will come from your air conditioner, so it's important to get one with sufficient capacity. You should calculate at least 3500 Btus per light. In this example, we show a ductless mini split A/C. The condenser is installed outside the room and connected by refrigerant lines to the air handling unit (AHU), which is mounted inside.

DEHUMIDIFIER (2)

When you're growing 6-9 plants, at their peak, they can transpire roughly 10 gallons of water per day. Unless you want to empty that reservoir in the morning and afternoon, you should opt for a dehumidifier with an 80-pint capacity. Be sure that your unit is positioned in such a way that it does not blow hot air directly onto the plants.

HORIZONTAL AIR FLOW (3)

See Open Air, Single Light (page 75).

LIGHT (4)

The same concepts we discussed in our Open-Air, Single-Light design—and at length in Chapter Three—apply here. Additionally, since your room is closed off from the outside, you run the risk of dramatic overheating should your air conditioner fail. Your best bet is purchase a temperature controller; you simply plug your lights in and, should they get too hot, it'll automatically shut them off.

WATER (5)

See Open Air, Single Light.

POT PLACEMENT (6)

See Open Air, Single Light.

PLANT SPACING (7) AND LIGHT FOOTPRINT (8)

See Open Air, Single Light.

CO$_2$ TANK AND REGULATOR (9)

Without the benefit of fresh air, a closed space requires you to provide all the carbon dioxide your plants need. Far and away the best option is a tank, regulator, and controller with a sensor. The sensor will monitor the CO$_2$ levels, and when they get too low, the controller will open the regulator and release CO$_2$ into the air. The CO$_2$ needs to mix with the air in the room—it shouldn't be blown directly into the canopy—so it's best to release it in the path of a fan. Make sure the emitter is far enough away from the sensor (hence the longer hose) or the regulator won't properly gauge your levels. We suggest purchasing a controller, sensor, and emitter that are designed to work tandem (they're often sold as packages).

SHOPPING LIST:

- **LIGHTS:** 600–1,000 W fixture, with timer

- **AIR:** 5000 Btu (minimum) mini split A/C unit; two small horizontal air flow fans

- **CO$_2$:** CO$_2$ tank, regulator, and controller (often purchased as a set)

- **GAUGES:** Thermostat and humidistat

- **HUMIDITY:** 80-pint dehumidifier

- **WATER:** Watering can

- **PLANTERS:** One 5–7 gallon pot for each of your seeds/ clones

- **INTERIOR:** White paint or sheets of Foylon/Mylar; a pallet, table, or something to keep your pots off the ground

4

OPEN AIR, FOUR LIGHTS

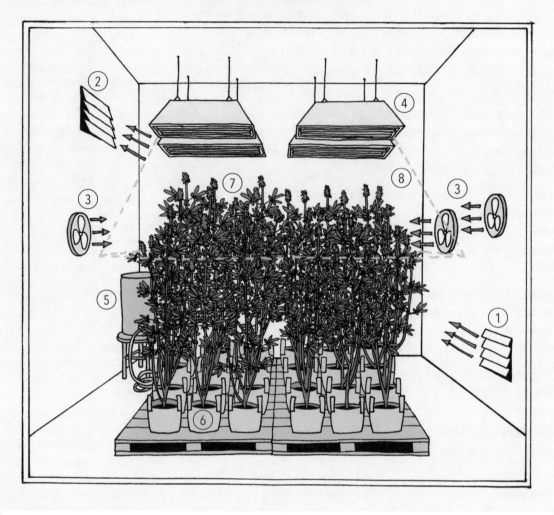

PROs

- Efficient use of resources
- Low startup costs
- Fresh air encourages a healthy microbiome
- Ability to grow multiple strains and introduce variety
- Easy to setup, add to, and adjust

CONs

- Weather can change conditions; you must be willing to adjust on the fly
- Possible exposure to pests from the outdoors
- Potential for heavy cannabis odors

INTAKE (1) / EXHAUST (2)

Just as in the single-light version of this setup, you're counting on fresh air to condition your garden. Ideally, you'd replace all of the air in the room twice every minute (though you can get away with less in cooler climates and seasons). Let's say your room is 10' x 10' x 8'—about the minimum size to for a 4-light setup—that is 800 cubic feet. This means you'll want an inline fan, connected to your exhaust, that can move at least 1600 cubic feet per minute.

HORIZONTAL AIR FLOW (3)

In this example, we recommend three fans. The two on the right are aligned just inside the edges of the canopy while the one on the left is centered. This arrangement creates two circles of air—the idea is they'll mix with each other and then separate, and the goal is to ensure the plants experience even temperatures and levels of CO_2.

LIGHTS (4)

The same principles that we've previously covered apply, but when working with multiple lights, you also have to consider their spacing. This will largely be determined by your choice of reflector, and you should follow the manufacturer's recommendations. (Be sure that you're buying a product that has thorough information regarding coverage).

Draw your layout on the floor before you start installing the hardware, and when determining your positions, always measure from the center of the bulb.

WATER (5)

For a garden this size, you may consider a water barrel and hose. Just be sure to position the barrel higher than the top of your pots so that gravity can do its work. We recommend a watering-wand attachment as well; it's helpful to get to the middle of your canopy without roughing up your plants.

POT PLACEMENT (6)

With a 4-light grid your canopy can stretch to 10' x 10'. Be sure to arrange your pots in such a way that you can access the center without too much trouble. If you want to maximize production, you can place your pots on casters to easily move them around while you work—otherwise, you can just leave a little extra space to move through. Another option is to add extra space between the lights, creating 4 separate islands of plant canopies. All of this depends, of course, on how much space you're working with.

PLANT SPACING (7) AND LIGHT FOOTPRINT (8)

In this example, the light footprint is based on the perimeter of the 4 lights.

As discussed above, depending on how you arrange your garden, this can vary dramatically, but the same principle applies: your canopy should occupy as much of the illuminated space as possible.

SHOPPING LIST:

- **LIGHTS:** Four 600–1,000 W fixtures, with timer (if using a single timer, be sure it has a sufficient amperage rating for all 4 lights)

- **AIR:** 4"–6" inline exhaust fan with 1600 CFM rating (and temperature-based controller); three small horizontal airflow fans

- **GAUGES:** Thermostat and humidistat

- **WATER:** Reservoir with hose and watering wand

- **PLANTERS:** One 5–7 gallon pot for each of your seeds/clones

- **INTERIOR:** White paint or sheets of Foylon/Mylar; a pallet, table, or something to keep your pots off the ground

CLOSED AIR, FOUR LIGHTS

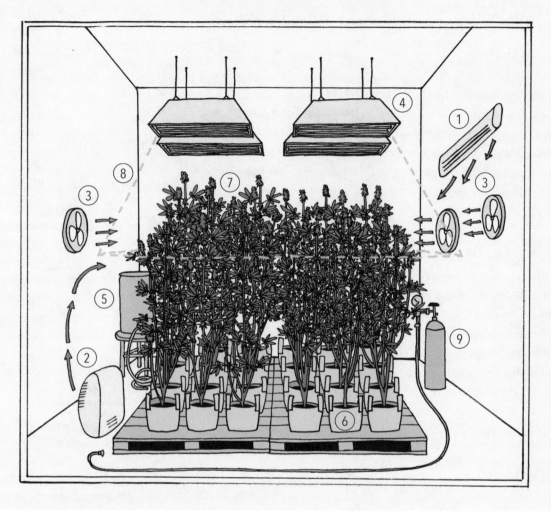

PROs

- High yielding
- Ability to grow multiple strains and introduce variety
- Once you're up and running, consistent and repeatable results
- Limits outside cannabis odor

CONs

- High startup costs
- Uses far more energy than an open-air garden
- If a piece of equipment fails, plants can dramatically suffer or die
- May take several cycles to land on perfect garden conditions

AIR CONDITIONER (1)

As in the closed-air, single-light setup (see page 77), the only way to properly air-condition this kind of environment is with a ductless system. Again, your grow room will require 3,500 Btus of cooling for every light, so you should opt for a unit with at least 14,000 Btus.

DEHUMIDIFIER (2)

The concept is the same as the closed-air, single-light setup, but a greater number of plants means significantly more transpiration. A 4-light setup will require, at its peak, roughly 250–300 pints of dehumidification per day. This can be accomplished with an industrial-strength unit or 2 smaller units (during some stages of growth, you'll likely only use 1).

HORIZONTAL AIR FLOW (3)

See Open Air, 4 Lights (page 79).

LIGHTS (4)

See Open Air, 4 Light.

WATER (5)

See Open Air, 4 Lights.

POT PLACEMENT (6)

See Open Air, 4 Lights.

PLANT SPACING (7) AND LIGHT FOOTPRINT (8)

See Open Air, 4 Lights.

CO_2 TANK AND REGULATOR (9)

See Closed Air, Single Light.

SHOPPING LIST:

- **LIGHTS:** Four 600–1,000 W fixtures, with timer (if using a single timer, be sure it has a sufficient amperage rating for all 4 lights)

- **AIR:** 20,000 Btu (minimum) mini split A/C

- **CO_2:** CO_2 tank, regulator and controller (often purchased as a set)

- **GAUGES:** Thermostat and humidistat

- **HUMIDITY:** Dehumidifier (or dehumidifiers) with a total capacity of 250–300 pints

- **WATER:** Reservoir with hose and watering wand

- **PLANTERS:** One 5–7 gallon pot for each of your seeds/clones

- **INTERIOR**: White paint or sheets of Foylon/Mylar; a pallet, table, or something to keep your pots off the ground

4

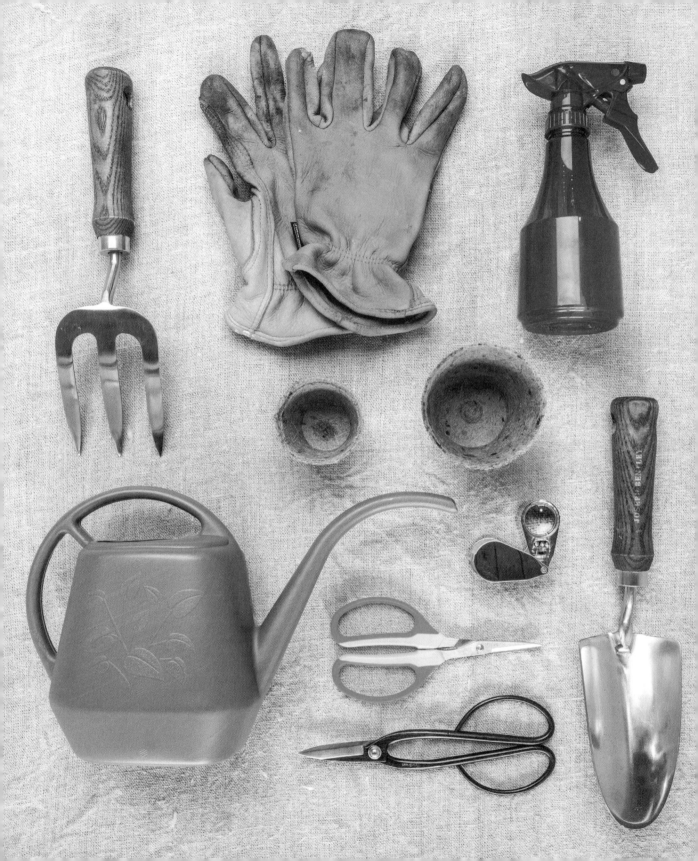

Chapter Five

TOOLS & EQUIPMENT

BY NOW YOU'VE HUNG YOUR LIGHTS, PAINTED YOUR WALLS, AND CONNECTED your fans. But before you get your hands dirty in the garden, you'll want to pick up a few tools to maintain it.

Unless you're diving headfirst into a big commercial grow operation, we always recommend starting small and scalable. For the most part, these tools are the same ones you'd use for any serious home gardening. Keep in mind that fine line between inexpensive and cheap. You can find great tools on Craigslist, in thrift stores, and at garage sales—items that won't set you back much and can last you a lifetime—but beware of the shoddily constructed $5 trowel that will break the third time you use it. When you've exhausted your secondhand options, hit up your local hardware store and plant nursery for the rest. You can browse the online cannabis retailers, but be warned that many of the cannabis-specific products—they're usually green and emblazoned with pot leaves—are made cheaply in China and serve no additional function.

And while we encourage frugality wherever possible, there's something to using tools that feel special to you. We have these beautiful Japanese scissors—they're heavy, copper, and feel great in your hand. Something about them just speaks to us. Find tools that are similarly well designed and constructed, and whatever hours you spend pruning and trimming the garden will feel less like a chore.

This chapter isn't meant to be a universal checklist; not every garden requires every tool, and once you get growing, you'll surely discover preferences of your own. Still, we hope this serves as a good jumping-off point, a handy resource while you're doing your shopping.

Tool & Equipment Recommendations

PH METER OR LITMUS PAPER

Generally, if you're growing in the kinds of soil we recommend, you won't need to constantly check your PH levels. Still, it's important to get occasional readings of your water's PH, just to make sure it's in the normal range (5.8–6.5 is ideal). For these purposes, a basic electronic PH meter will do (and you shouldn't need to shell out more than $40 or so). If you're using a hydroponic system, you'll need to adjust the PH of your nutrient solutions with every watering, so it's worth investing in one of the kits designed specifically for those purposes.

PROPAGATION TRAYS

When you buy propagation trays from a nursery, they usually look something like large, black ice-cube molds or muffin tins. But at the scale of most home grows, you can use just about anything to hold your clones and seedlings while they're developing roots—a Dixie cup, a mason jar, an old yogurt container. Just avoid anything that previously contained toxic chemicals, and steer clear of stainless steel, as it kills helpful bacteria.

SEED-STARTING PLUGS

While your seeds and clones are developing roots, it's critical that they're in a medium that holds both moisture and nutrients and allows for easy root penetration. We use rock-wool cubes, which are made from a mineral wool, but Root Riot makes a starter cube from composted organic material that also ensures a balance of water and oxygen and encourages root growth. In either case, when it comes time to transfer your plants into a pot, the seed starter can be buried right along with it.

POTS

The size of your pots will likely be determined by the size of your grow space—we'd caution against anything under 3 gallons, but the more room you give those roots, the better. We prefer fabric pots over plastic or ceramic, as they're breathable, which is great for your soil (and thus great for your plants).

SUPPORT

As they grow bigger and start to flower, most cannabis plants will need some help standing upright. Sativa-dominant strains tend to need a little more support, and some particularly stout indicas may be fine on their own, but you'll have a better idea of what will suffice as your individual plants develop. Good options include bamboo stakes, tomato cages, cotton netting, and tie wires. There are cannabis-specific supports on the market, but we haven't found them necessary (or significantly more helpful than standard gardening products).

SPRAY BOTTLE OR PLANT MISTER

You can find handsome options in the beauty aisle of your local supermarket or something sturdy in janitorial supplies, but so long as you're not reusing containers of chemical spray, just about any bottle will do. You'll want one for water and several for cleaning solutions, so be sure they're clearly marked.

CLEANER

We highly recommend cleaning with d-limonene—a terpene that's already present in cannabis. When we're cleaning our tools, we use it straight and uncut, either from a spray bottle or a mason jar—something with a wide mouth that makes it easy to wet a rag. For a gentler all-purpose cleaner, combine one part d-limonene

STICKY SITUATION

If you've ever had to scrub pine sap from your hands, you'll have an idea of what it's like working with cannabis resin. No matter how fastidious you are, during harvest, just about everything that crosses the threshold of your grow room ends up sticky. And though it may seem like it after many hours in the the garden, resin isn't there just to gunk up your tools, fingers, faucet handles, and doorknobs; in nature it serves several important purposes. It's produced and secreted by the trichomes of the plant, largely as a defense mechanism against nonbeneficial insects, which have a hard time getting to the plant matter due to that sticky barrier (plus, many pests find the aroma offensive). It's also a natural antifungal and an effective line of defense against some of Mother Nature's more destructive forces: low humidity, high wind, and UVB rays. And we humans, of course, appreciate the resin because it contains a significant amount of the cannabinoids and terpenes we find so pleasurable and healing. Our garden tools, however, suffer the consequences. They do our dirty work and thus need regular TLC and maintenance.

After each use, clean your tools to ensure they're not permanently gummed up. Many growers opt for olive or coconut oil—just pour a dab of it on a washcloth and go to town. We've converted to d-limonene for our cleaning needs (which sharp readers will recognize from our discussion of terpenes in Chapter Two). It's crazy powerful, completely natural—extracted from the rinds of lemons, limes, and oranges—and the secret ingredient in most citrus-based cleaners.

It won't come as a surprise that we oppose harsh synthetic cleaners—your tools and surfaces will interact with the plant matter, which, if all goes well, you'll end up inhaling or ingesting—but we'd also caution against store-bought "natural" ones. Even the organic brands have heavy scents that can affect your finished product. You're going through a lot of trouble to develop nuanced flavors in your cannabis—don't ruin them with your choice of cleaning products.

and one part water, then add a couple drops of liquid soap. You might also keep a jar of olive or coconut oil handy. Both are great for getting resin off your tools, and a little bit on your fingers makes trimming much easier. Isopropyl alcohol is a slightly cheaper option for your cleaning needs; just be sure not to spray any on your plants, bud, or trim.

SHEARS

In general, pruning shears are used for stems and trimming shears are used for leaves, but in an indoor cannabis garden, you may find a single high-quality pair of the latter can handle most of your needs. (If you do spring for pruning shears, go for something small—you're not going to be lopping off an oak branch.) The best shears we've found are made for trimming bonsais; they have a small point that's perfect for detail work, and their non-stick coating helps prevent resin buildup.

GLOVES

During trimming and harvesting, you may find you want a barrier between that sticky resin and your hands. Disposable latex or nitrile gloves work great (the latter are synthetic, and a great alternative if you have latex allergies), but in either case, go for the nonpowdered variety. And even when wearing gloves, we recommend rubbing your fingers with a dab of olive oil to counteract the resin.

JEWELER'S LOUPE

When it comes time to monitor the development of your trichomes, you'll need to get a closer look. Unlike a microscope, a jeweler's loupe is easy to carry around the grow room and lets you monitor the buds while they're still on the plant. A 20x magnification will do, but 40x is ideal—do yourself a favor and opt for a model with a built-in LED light.

SHOVEL/TROWEL

You won't be doing any heavy digging in an indoor garden—no need to break the bank on this front—but you'll need a small hand shovel to scoop soil and amendments into your pots.

DRYING SETUP

Your drying space will depend on the size and number of your plants. If you're growing just one or two, a couple of wire hangers or a clothesline will do. A few more and you may want a collapsible drying rack.

STAY SHARP

Even if you can't find a pair of exquisite Japanese shears, whatever you use to prune your plants should have a sharp, clean edge. Dull tools will mangle your plants and increase the odds of infection and contamination. A compromised plant spends energy healing its wounds rather than growing big and strong and developing its flowers. A power grinder is most effective, but in the spirit of starting small and scalable, a whetstone will do just fine (and usually runs you $10–$20). If you're not quite comfortable grinding and filing, most local hardware stores will sharpen your shears for a small fee—watch a pro until you're DIY-ready.

CURING CONTAINERS

We use BPA-free 5-gallon buckets with twist-off lids, but on a smaller scale, glass jars often make the most sense (if the jars are clear glass, be careful to store them out of direct light). Make sure that whatever container you use is nonporous, disinfected, and free of lingering smells. (We'll discuss curing containers in more detail in Chapter Nine.)

DIGITAL KITCHEN SCALE

It's important to be sure you're staying in compliance with state regulations by weighing your cured flower, but a digital scale is also useful for getting the right doses in edibles and tinctures. Be sure to find something that measures in grams.

MEASURING CUPS

You'll want quick and accurate measurements of your liquid nutrients, and while liquid measuring cups will do, we've found bartender's mixing glasses—those pints with graduated markings—to be the most convenient. Best to clearly mark a designated glass for each solution, and flush with water after each use.

ONCE A CANNABIS TOOL, ALWAYS A CANNABIS TOOL

Designating tools as cannabis-only means you'll never have to go hunting around your home—they'll always be right where you need them. More importantly, garden tools that come into contact with soil nutrients, which are rarely food-grade, should never be invited into your kitchen. You keep your cleaning fluids, buckets, and brushes separate from those for cooking, right? Do yourself a favor and follow suit in the garden.

5

Chapter Six

GROW
MEDIUMS

FEED YOUR SOIL, NOT YOUR PLANTS.

That's something of a mantra around our grow rooms and among like-minded cultivators. Whereas many farmers—not only in the cannabis world, but in commercial agriculture as a whole—identify the nutrient requirements of a plant, then meet those needs with chemical fertilizers, we believe deeply in a natural order. If you take care of your plants' ecosystem, that ecosystem will in turn take care of your plants.

When cannabis grows the old-fashioned way, it absorbs its nutrients from organic material that naturally decomposes into a simple water-soluble form. It benefits from a host of microorganisms living in the soil, breaking down and delivering the nitrogen, phosphorous, potassium, and other micronutrients that the plant needs to grow. These microorganisms also help protect plants from disease and harmful pests. Your job, then, is to make sure these communities of micro-allies have what they need to flourish.

The bulk of this chapter is dedicated to exploring the principles of living soil and offering practical advice, instructions, and even nutrient recipes that will help you create a healthy, sustainable environment where your plants will thrive. But soil—at least as we're using the term (a careful calibration of organic ingredients and mineral particles, not just any old dirt from the ground)—is not the only available grow medium. We'll also walk you through a simple off-the-rack solution that will help you get started, and we'll introduce you to a couple of popular alternative models.

Hydroponics & Aeroponics

While we might prefer gardening gloves to lab coats, there's more than one way to get your plants the nutrients they need. Plenty of quality cannabis is grown by alternative methods that bypass live earth entirely. Hydroponic systems are probably the most popular. In this technique, the plants' roots are supported by an inert medium—often rockwool, perlite, or coco coir—and given a highly controlled formula of liquid or powdered nutrients.

Hydroponic cannabis usually grows faster and more efficiently; the plant expends very little energy searching for nutrients in the ground, and instead directs it toward leaf and flower production. And it can certainly be a space saver, as the plants require smaller root systems. There are growers for whom a hydroponic system is without a doubt the best option. But when choosing your method of growing you should weigh both process and end result. And the end result of hydroponic growing tends to be a fairly homogenous one. This isn't always a bad thing: mass-produced medical cannabis is well-served by guaranteed reproducible results. But it's difficult to reproduce the sophisticated and complex flavors, aromas, and effects that soil provides. The ecosystem of the soil caters to the plant's nutrient needs, which, in many ways, makes the process more forgiving—with hydroponic systems it's entirely up to the grower.

Aeroponic systems bypass grow mediums entirely: cannabis roots are fully exposed, and are misted with water and nutrient solutions. This method requires a tightly controlled environment—if there's an outbreak of any sort of disease, mold, or harmful pest, the plants are highly susceptible in their compromised state. While this method may seem like the most futuristic of the bunch—it is, after all, what's allowed NASA to grow produce in zero gravity—it's actually been around since the sixties, and it's becoming more and more prevalent in very small, portable systems and in clone rooms.

Our hearts and hands remain in the soil—and as such, so do most of this book's recommendations—but there are numerous setups for these kinds of systems, and if you've got the expendable income, technical proficiency, and a little curiosity, there are a number of great retailers that can help outfit you with what you need.

Prefab Soils

If you're looking for a low barrier to entry—at least in terms of labor—you're probably best served by purchasing bagged organic potting soil along with a nutrient blend, which come in both dry and liquid varieties. This is the most common starting point for home growers—particularly at a smaller scale—and a great way to hone your skills without being overwhelmed by the process. In the long run, our preference is for a more holistic living-soil approach—which we'll get to next—but this route is effective, produces consistent results, and provides a solid foundation for more sophisticated methods (which you can always transition to once you get your feet wet).

Over time and at a larger scale, purchasing potting soil and nutrients can get expensive. It's also less environmentally friendly, and, if and when you have to customize your nutrient solutions, it may require a bit more chemistry than many home gardeners prefer. That said, most first-time growers take this grab-and-go tack and enjoy great success. There's certainly no shame in buying a bag or two of soil and getting started.

Ask a salesperson to recommend a good organic product. (On this front, you'll probably have better luck at a local nursery than a big-box store.) Your soil should have adequate drainage, a healthy amount of nutrients, and no toxic insecticides, pesticides, or chemical fertilizers. Scan the ingredient list and look for earthworm castings, seabird guano, fish bone meal, kelp meal, oyster shell flour, dolomitic lime, gypsum, and mycorrhizae. You also want ingredients that create the right texture and aid in water retention: perlite, pumice, vermiculite, and coconut coir are all on-target. Avoid soils geared toward specific types of cultivation (say, blends for cacti and succulents or African violets), and go for something general-purpose and nutrient rich.

If your potting soil is packed with beneficial nutrients and minerals—and a good deal of them are slow-releasing—then you're probably safe to transfer it directly into your pots without initial additives. Otherwise, plan to supplement your soil with a vegetative nutrient blend. These are high in nitrogen and potassium, but contain phosphorus as well.

In either case, you want to add further nutrients at the onset of flowering. (See Chapter Seven.) Bloom nutrients, as they're usually known, are typically low in nitrogen and high in phosphorus and potassium. (This lines up with your plants' intake as they start to develop flowers.) Bloom blends should include a wide array of microbes and mycorrhizae: *Pisolithus tinctorius*, *Scleroderma citrinum*, and *Rhizopogon luteolus*, among others.

Just as with potting soil, there are all sorts of nutrients on the market; we recommend springing for something high-quality, organic, and specifically crafted for cannabis. Whether you're using liquid or powdered varieties—and the latter tend to be cheaper—nutrient blends vary widely in density and potency, so defer to the manufacturer's application instructions. Not all nutrients are created equal; not every manufacturer knows how to make a quality product; and even among those that do, not everyone is invested in doing so responsibly. Ask for recommendations from friends and nursery employees alike. Look for manufacturers that provide certified lab-tested results and can explain their products in simple terms. Seek out OMRI or USDA Organic labels—while this doesn't guarantee a good product, it does mean that the methods of manufacturing are vetted by a third party with environmental quality in mind. Once you find a product you like, stick with that manufacturer. Odds are, a good nutrient line has complementary products, and its maker has most likely refined and tested those products side by side.

HOW MUCH DO I NEED?

Most potting soil comes in large plastic bags that are 8-quart, 16-quart, 32-quart, or 1½ or 2 cubic feet in capacity. A quality 2-cubic-foot bag of organic potting soil will run you anywhere from $15–$40; a 32-quart bag is usually $10–$25. If you're trying to decide how much soil you need to fill your pots—assuming you're planting a root ball or clone cube and that you need not fill your pot to the brim—here's a little cheat sheet:

3-GALLON POT ≈

⅓ CUBIC FOOT OF SOIL or 10 DRY QUARTS

5-GALLON POT ≈

½ CUBIC FOOT OF SOIL or 16 DRY QUARTS

10-GALLON POT ≈

1 CUBIC FOOT OF SOIL or 32 DRY QUARTS

25-GALLON POT ≈

3 CUBIC FEET OF SOIL or 96 DRY QUARTS

Living Soils

A comprehensive manual for creating healthy living soils would quickly eclipse the book you're holding. It's a complex practice, and can take many years to master. Still, we believe it's not only best for your plants but also the most sustainable and ethical method of farming. Healthy living soils help to regulate water needs; reduce the potential for disease and pests (and thus negate the need for harmful pesticides); and increase the potential for nutrient cycling, which means relying less on expensive and ecologically questionable fertilizer products. Healthy living soils also encourage an increase in yield and growth rate—something we're sure you won't complain about. This is an intricate science, and even on our end, a process of trial and error. We're fortunate to have a talented, thoughtful consultant helping us with our soil at Raven, and thought this chapter—not to mention your homegrown cannabis—would benefit from his expertise as well. What follows is based on concepts put forth by Raskal Turbeville, a mycologist and soil biologist from Ojai, California.

WHAT IS SOIL?

Well . . . soil is the ground beneath our feet and a key resource for creating and sustaining life on this planet. It's responsible for providing our food and for the plants that create our oxygen. As water passes through the ground toward the aquifers, it is cleansed of toxins and metals, aided by plant roots and other biota. Soil is a major component of carbon sequestration, and a key factor in our efforts to reduce the effects of greenhouse gas emissions. Soil is the home for a complex web of organisms that makes life on this planet possible, and if our intention is to grow healthy plants, it's essential that we understand soil's part in that process.

In less lofty terms, soil is an amalgamation of sand, silt, and clay. These components vary in particle size—sand is the largest, followed by silt, and then clay—and their ratio determines what we call the "texture" of the soil. Texture is a critical factor: A sand-heavy soil will have increased drainage—which can be beneficial for some plants—but less nutrient retention. A clay-heavy soil will retain water well and earn high marks for nutrient retention, but might not allow a plant's roots the oxygen they need. Ideally, all three components will be present in roughly equal measure: this is called a "loam soil."

Organic matter and minerals are likewise key ingredients—not only do they aid the physical structure of soil, but they also act as parent material for the nutrients your plants consume to grow and thrive. This leads to the last piece of the puzzle: the microbiome, the community of microorganisms that live in the soil and form a symbiotic relationship with plants. Many of the essential processes and functions of soil are mediated by this micro-universe.

6

THE SOIL FOOD WEB

If we made the microbiome sound like some egalitarian hippie utopia, know that it's also akin to a postapocalyptic landscape, an intricate chain of who eats whom. Everyone is eating someone or, for that matter, what's left of them. This is how energy is exchanged and how nutrients end up in the soil. The chain starts with the primary producers: plants, algae, lichen, and certain bacteria that photosynthesize and fix carbon dioxide using the sun's energy. They're assisted by bacteria and mycorrhizal fungi, which help cycle water and nutrients to their host. These organisms live on or around the plant, expanding its capacity for survival and adaptation. As plants shed their leaves and die, they become food for the decomposers—bacteria, fungi, and pathogenic and parasitic organisms—which eat and excrete waste. This waste is then consumed by another group of decomposers. And then there are the protozoa and nematodes—predators of the soil—which feed on living bacteria and fungi. This goes on and on. But as the web grows larger and more intricate, its constituents are also breaking down organic material into bioavailable forms that can be used by plants. The intricacies of the soil food web may never be fully grasped, but the more we learn, the more we understand how we can partner with our micro-allies for healthy soil and healthy plants.

THE CONVENTIONAL AGRICULTURE APPROACH

In conventional farming—as in modern medicine—there's been a tendency to view microorganisms as a liability, not an asset. Instead of harnessing the benefits of the soil food web—working with the microbiome

COMPANION PLANTS

Companion plants encourage a greater diversity of microorganisms, help ward off pests, and fix nitrogen in your soil. Just be sure to choose a plant that won't compete for root space. Our top recommendation for an indoor garden is clover: it's nitrogen fixing, grows right on the surface of the soil, and can help to protect your plants from fungus gnats. (Other nitrogen-fixing plants—like alfalfa, vetch, and ryegrass—are great for outdoor growing, but take a little more work, as they need to be cut back regularly.) Many garden herbs—thyme, basil, marigolds, mint—produce compounds that help to deter insects. (And why not let your grow room double as an herb garden?) If you're thinking of making cannabis topicals, you'll be well served by rosemary and calendula.

to protect against potentially harmful pests and pathogens—we tend to sterilize the soil and then attempt to reintroduce particular nutrients and minerals.

Tilling, a breakthrough in modern food production, is one of the major disturbances to soil ecology. As we tear into the ground, communities of microorganisms are ripped apart and the structure of the soil is lost, leaving it vulnerable to compaction. Soil is resilient, and communities can regain a foothold in their native environment, but tilling year after year will eventually lead to a great loss of diversity and health. A broken soil food web opens the door to pests and diseases, which in turn encourages the use of harmful pesticides. The "remedies" we implement to hinder unwanted visitors often

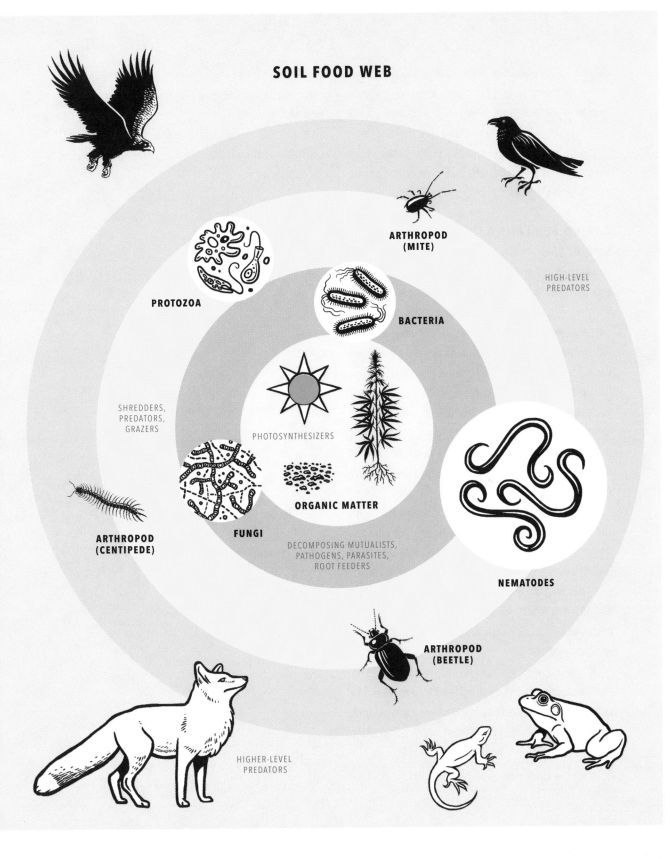

SOIL FOOD WEB

HIGH-LEVEL PREDATORS

ARTHROPOD (MITE)

PROTOZOA

BACTERIA

SHREDDERS, PREDATORS, GRAZERS

PHOTOSYNTHESIZERS

ORGANIC MATTER

ARTHROPOD (CENTIPEDE)

FUNGI

DECOMPOSING MUTUALISTS, PATHOGENS, PARASITES, ROOT FEEDERS

NEMATODES

ARTHROPOD (BEETLE)

HIGHER-LEVEL PREDATORS

contain compounds that are poisonous to our plants and make it difficult for populations of microorganisms to rebound. And without them, we're stuck using fertilizers that can harm both the plants and the long-term health of the soil. If we learn to work with soil rather than against it, it will mean less labor for us and a more harmonious environment for our plants.

CARING FOR LIVING SOIL

So where does this leave the home cannabis grower? If you're working with a few planters in your basement, you probably weren't planning on tilling per se. But the principle is the same: aim for as little soil disturbance as possible. You needn't empty your pots between harvests; you needn't break the soil apart. Even the roots from your previous plant are beneficial—your new plant's roots will intertwine with the old ones, gaining access to their microbial activity, and roots can serve as passageways for water and air. You'll simply pull out the stalk of your old plant—much of the root mass will come along with it—and plant the new one in its place.

Larger pots help to encourage a richer soil food web. The more space, the more capacity for microorganisms. Larger pots also allow for companion plants, which can help to create a more diverse ecosystem. We also advocate mulching organic matter right on top of the soil, as this helps retain moisture levels and provides your microbial community with food. A bare surface lends itself to degradation.

When you're growing perpetually indoors, it can be hard to sustain a no-till method. But if you're willing to spring for a couple sets of pots, we have a simple trick that will let you mimic the winter months and allow your soil to recover. Each time you harvest, simply plant some nitrogen-fixing companions, add a layer of compost and amendments to the surface, and let that pot sit out a cycle. By rotating your pots, you can keep your soil healthy without pressing the pause button on your cannabis garden.

Compost

Compost is simply organic matter that has been broken down by microorganisms. Plants live, die, are consumed, and are expelled. Worms and bacteria weave their way through layers of manure, cycling nutrients and proliferating their populations. Natural ecologies build healthy soil through an ongoing process of production and decomposition. This is what we should seek to mimic.

Finished compost is one of the most important inputs you can make for your soil. It contains a diverse and abundant set of microorganisms, including bacteria, fungi, and protozoa. In a single handful of high-quality compost there are billions of microbes participating in the process of decomposition, and that process is creating micro- and macronutrients in forms that are readily available for your plants. It also forms a substance known as humus. Humus aids in soil structure, provides a home for microbial communities, acts as a long-term source of nutrients, and increases your soil's water retention. Compost is the starter culture for your soil's ecology, but it can be repeatedly applied to maintain and expand the microbiome during and between plantings.

There are numerous methods of composting, and each one will give you a slightly different end result. Worm composting is fairly easy and consistent; cold composting saves you a lot of work; and thermal composting has the advantage of being ready to use within a month. The process involves creating a pile of organic material, turning the pile based on its temperature, and maintaining consistent and balanced moisture levels.

CHOOSING YOUR MATERIALS

Your organic material must consist of a particular ratio of carbon to nitrogen, also referred to as "brown to green." Brown, woody material is usually your carbon source—branches, fallen leaves, dried plant stalks, etc. Nitrogen-rich material is organic matter that still retains its green color—grass clippings, newly fallen leaves, kitchen scraps. You'll need higher levels of nitrogen as well; this primarily comes from animal waste, seeds, nitrogen-fixing plants (think alfalfa or clover), as well as blood and organ meat. We suggest starting with

- 6 parts brown/carbon
- 3 parts green/nitrogen
- 1 part high-nitrogen

Remember to avoid plant materials that have been exposed to pesticides, chemicals, or other environmental toxins; they can be detrimental to the very microbial communities you are trying to proliferate. Choose material from a clean site and avoid GMOs whenever possible: their compounds are often designed to hinder microbial life. When using animal inputs, avoid anything with heavy levels of antibiotics, growth hormones, or GMO feed. And while blood and organs are great sources of nitrogen, if you're composting in an urban setting, expect them to attract rodents and other mammals. Be aware that many citrus and coniferous materials have high levels of antimicrobial oils. If they're your best option, let them sit for a couple of months before adding to your compost pile—eventually, those volatile compounds will leech out.

BUILDING AND TURNING YOUR PILE

Before you create your pile, it's important to pay attention to your moisture levels; most of the time, you're best served wetting down your browns and greens beforehand. Ideally, your moisture content will be in the range of 50–60%. (If you grab a handful of the compost material, it should feel like a wrung-out sponge, expelling just a few drops of water when squeezed.) As you start the turning process, you can add moisture to maintain consistency.

Your pile should measure at least 1 cubic yard, and the three categories of material should be evenly distributed throughout. Once your pile is in place, it will begin to heat up; this is due to a metabolic process—microbes growing, proliferating, eating, and dying. Your goal is to get the internal temperature to 160°F. (If you don't have a compost thermometer, use a meat thermometer and take temperature readings from the middle of the pile.) If the internal temperature rises above 165°F or drops below 155°F, your pile should be turned with a pitchfork; most of the decomposition is happening in the middle, so when you turn your pile, you want to transfer the outer layers into the middle. After one month—and four or so turns—your compost should be ready. Depending on the materials you started with, there may still be organic material present; you can simply sift it out. Spread your compost on a tarp, at a depth of no more than one foot, and allow it to cool for 24 hours before using.

TROUBLESHOOTING

If your pile fails to reach 160°F—either when you build it or after any of your four turns—it usually signifies a shortage of nitrogen in your pile. (The brown material is your fuel and the green is your fire: if you don't have enough fire, your fuel won't burn efficiently.) Try increasing the levels of nitrogen-rich materials incrementally, and see if you can get the temperature up. If your compost is heavy on dry organic matter, this is a sign that moisture levels were not maintained throughout the process. Re-wet your pile to that 50–60% level each time you turn it. Keep your pile out of direct sun and heavy winds—both can dry it out. If you live in a climate with a prolonged rainy season, it would be wise to compost in a covered area. And if, while turning, you are revolted by the smell, it's probably a sign of anaerobic growth; you'd be prudent to toss the compost and restart the process.

ASSESSING COMPOST

To get a thorough read on your compost, you'll need a decent microscope and a working knowledge of microbiology. That said, with thermal compost, where we're trying to proliferate and maintain a purely aerobic microbiome, there are some macro characteristics that will give you a pretty good idea of the quality. (These tips are helpful when gauging the quality of store-bought compost as well.)

- Your compost should smell sweet, earthy, and inviting. If you're getting a foul, putrid smell, it's a good indication that the microbial community has moved into an anaerobic state.
- The texture should be fluffy. If you squeeze it in your hand, it should form together; if you prod it with your finger, it should break apart.
- If the compost is slimy and waterlogged, there is a good chance it's been exposed to detrimental anaerobic organisms.
- The color should be dark brown (compare it to a bar of 80% dark chocolate). Black coloring is another indication that it's become anaerobic.

COMPOST TEA

While compost itself works wonders for your soil food web, it requires a lot of time and energy and may not go so far, even spread at a depth of only an inch. Compost tea—essentially an aerated, water-based concentrate—takes a small amount of your compost and exponentially expands the diversity and abundance of microorganism populations in your soil. Five gallons of high-quality tea can effectively inoculate a whole acre. If this seems like a no-brainer, take heed: for all its benefits, compost tea can quickly turn anaerobic. And if anaerobic protozoa are added to your soil, they'll clash with your aerobic biomes and quickly undo much of your hard work.

The process of making compost tea is relatively straightforward. Place your compost in a mesh bag, suspend it in actively aerated water, and feed the microorganism populations. Over the next day or two, the soil microbes will proliferate, expanding the population to whatever your given volume of water holds. Still, there are plenty of variables to keep in mind: water quality, temperature, starting material, bubble size, circulation, brewing time, dissolved oxygen content, cleanliness of your brewing vessel, and the type of food you add to the mix. Again—even for experienced brewers—this will take some trial and error.

Compost teas can be tailored to the specific type of microorganisms you wish to cultivate: for a bacteria-dominant tea, you'll want simple sugars; if you want to encourage fungal communities, it's best to use carbohydrates. As you become more familiar with the process, you might start to specialize, but at the outset, we recommend using unsulphured blackstrap molasses. It offers consistent results with less risk of anaerobic growth. Your ratios will depend on the quality of your compost, but 5–10 mL of molasses and 300–400 mL of compost per gallon of water is a good place to start.

Your tea can be added to the soil—just include it in your watering regimen—or sprayed directly onto the plant's leaves (this is called "foliar application"). You'll want to discontinue foliar application when your plants reach flowering growth.

The only way to be certain that your tea is encouraging beneficial aerobic biomes—not detrimental anaerobic ones—is with a microscope; if you plan to make a habit of brewing compost tea, it may be worth the investment. But short of a microscope, your nose is your best guide. Compost tea should smell sweet and earthy. If your tea smells like mildew or a wet dog, there's a good chance that things have turned anaerobic. You should also pay attention to what's called the "head." As microorganisms proliferate, bubbles will form on the

6

surface of the water. An ideal aerobic tea will often have a fluffy white head—similar to a bubble bath. An anaerobic tea will usually produce a brown biofilm. But even tea that exhibits positive traits could be suffering from the beginning of anaerobic growth, and such growth can continue when the tea is added to the soil. We say this not to scare you, but just so you're aware of potential consequences. When you get it right, your soil (and your plants) will certainly thank you.

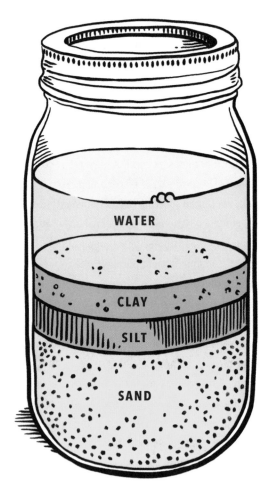

SOIL TEXTURE TEST

Before you add your native soil, it's helpful to determine its ratio of sand, silt, and clay. Generally you're looking for equal parts of each, but when growing in pots, it's helpful to keep your loam soil a bit on the sandy side—this helps with drainage. An easy way to determine your soil makeup is with a jar test.

1. Place a representative scoop of your soil in a quart-size mason jar; you want about 2 inches of dirt.

2. Fill the jar with water—leaving about 2 inches of room at the top—screw the lid on tightly, shake vigorously for 3 minutes, then place on a flat surface.

3. After a minute, the sand will have settled to the bottom. Using a Sharpie, mark the top of the sand line on the side of your jar.

4. After an hour, the silt will have settled on top of the sand. Make a second mark at the top of your silt line.

5. After a week, all of the clay should be settled on top of the silt. Make a third mark. (There will likely be some organic matter still floating in the jar, so don't expect your water to be clear.)

6. Measure the depth of each layer to calculate the ratio of sand/silt/clay.

Soil Mixtures

BASIC SOIL MIXTURE

The complex litany of inputs for some soil mixes can look like something out of *Mastering the Art of French Cooking*, and getting just the right balance of nutrients, minerals, textures, and microorganisms works wonders for your plants. Still, a good, simple mix can go a long way, and by treating it right over time, you'll end up with a wonderfully hospitable ecosystem. The basic soil recipe calls for equal parts compost and native soil.

The compost acts as your microbial starter while the native soil aids in developing structure and drainage. Mix them together and wet them to a 50–60% moisture level. (Remember: This should feel something like a wrung-out sponge. When you squeeze the mixture in your hand, it should let out only a couple of drops of water.)

You want to harvest native soil from a fertile place—a garden bed or a productive lawn—and it's best to take from the top 6 inches. Take care to avoid soils that could be contaminated with toxic material or heavy metals. Remember that you're looking for a loam texture. If you don't have access to native soil, you can substitute a potting mix—these are usually in the loam category, and contain ingredients like perlite to increase drainage.

INTERMEDIATE SOIL MIXTURE

Building off your basic mix, you can increase the potential for microbial abundance by adding a few more inputs. Keep the amount of compost in your mix at 50%, but reduce your native soil to 35%. You'll balance this out by adding 10% biochar and 5% high-nitrogen material.

Biochar is a specialized form of charcoal made from a range of feedstock—usually plant matter. Due to its porous surface, biochar provides excellent housing for microbial communities and helps soil retain both water and nutrients. It's important to use biochar that has been activated with nutrient sources (such as fish hydrolysate). If you're activating your own biochar, you can tailor the ingredients to account for any deficiencies in the soil.

High-nitrogen materials help promote growth in general, but particularly when it comes to heavy-feeding plants like cannabis. Animal manure is a popular input—just be sure that it comes from animals that have not been given growth hormones or pesticide-saturated feed. Nitrogen-fixing plants, such as clover and alfalfa, are also effective.

To compensate for the lack of native soil, you might also add a cup of mineral additives—rock dust is the most common, but we advocate using shell-based materials, as they don't rely on unsustainable mining practices.

Once you've gathered your inputs, mix them together and aim for that same 50–60% moisture level.

6

SOIL PYRAMID

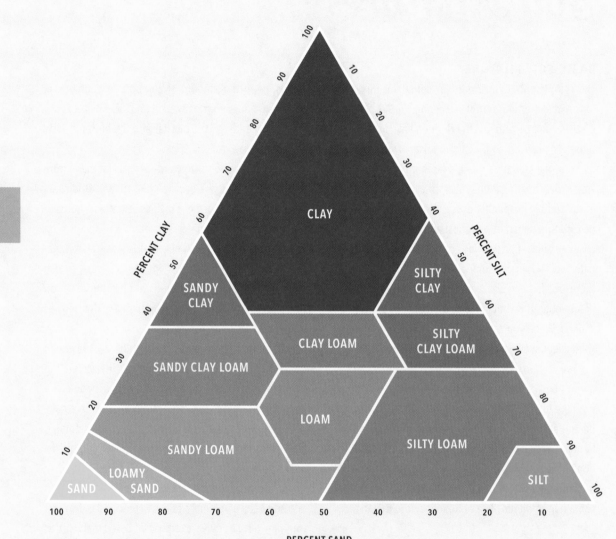

Microorganism & Nutrient Inputs

The conventional approach to growing crops calls for dumping large quantities of fertilizer on your plants in order to obtain a high yield. Not only are these fertilizers expensive, but they often contain ingredients that are actually detrimental to soil ecology. What's more, without a proper microbial community supporting it, a plant can take up only a small fraction of the fertilizer—most of it ends up as runoff in the water. The truth is, the microbial community is able to be much more attentive to our plants' needs than we will ever be. Still, for those of us who love to tinker, we can craft specific nutrient solutions to feed both our micro-allies and our beloved plants.

The recipes in this section have been adapted from the practice of Korean natural farming and have been passed on to Raskal by individuals connected to that practice. This method is based on the theory that indigenous microorganisms have evolved under local conditions and alongside local food sources, and thus are best suited for the local environment. The diversity you find just by walking into the forest and digging near the base of a tree is far greater than anything you can buy in a store. (It's also free!) The science of creating these inputs is still incomplete and requires careful observation and a willingness to experiment. Our aim is to give you a basic understanding of how to start working with microbial cultivation, and in doing so, help you raise healthy and bountiful cannabis.

WATER

Before we get into specific microbial and nutrient solutions, we want to emphasize the importance of water quality. The water you use should be free of pollutants and toxins and untreated with any chemicals that may deter microorganisms. Your best options are natural sources—springwater is not only pure in form but also high in mineral content; rainwater is likewise excellent for these solutions. If you are using municipal water sources, check to see if they are treated with chlorine or chloramine, which can inhibit microbial diversity and growth. Chlorine can be off-gassed: just let the water sit

GROW YOUR OWN MICROORGANISMS

If you don't have access to native soil, you can still foster local communities of microorganisms. Gather some organic material—grass, leaves, etc.—wet it down, and cover it with a tarp. After a week or two you will begin to see the white threads of fungi: this is a sign that you've cultivated a microecology. Expand your microbial diversity by choosing various food sources from various locations. The more diverse the microbial population, the better. (As always, avoid materials that have been exposed to pesticides.)

in an open container for 24 hours. Chloramine will not off-gas, but can be made inert with one drop of humic acid for each gallon. Humic acid can be purchased or made from compost—simply take your finished compost, place it in a mesh bag, and pour water through it. If the liquid on the other end comes out dark brown (again, it should look like a bar of 80% dark chocolate), you should be golden. If the liquid is a lighter color, you may need to increase the dilution rate to effectively bind up the chloramine.

TEMPERATURE AND LIGHT

While storing your solutions at a temperature of 85-90°F will maximize the growth rate of your microbial inputs, it won't keep them in pristine quality. Your cannabis plants won't experience such heat on a consistent basis, and your goal should be to prepare microorganisms for the conditions and temperatures your plants are facing. So long as the water stays above 65°F—any colder and you'll inhibit microbial activity—ambient temperature will foster effective microbial communities.

Similarly, in their natural environment, microbial communities are protected from the harsh rays of the sun, which can inhibit or kill microorganisms and degrade nutrient content. Do yourself a favor: make and store your solutions out of direct sunlight.

SOLUTION CONTAINERS

When making (and storing) microbial and nutrient inputs, it's best to use glass, ceramic, or plastic containers. Stay away from metals like stainless steel, as they often have antimicrobial properties and may inhibit growth. The same goes for any utensils used to stir your solutions.

Local Microbiome Solution

An excellent starter for cultivating a diverse soil ecology—and boost for your microbial communities—this solution uses the local microorganisms you've been collecting. It captures a wide range of bacteria, fungi, and predator organisms that profoundly increase the quality of your soil. Note that the diversity of the final product is dependent on the diversity of the materials you choose.

INGREDIENTS:

4 ½ gallons chlorine and chloramine-free water

2 oz. (about ¼ cup unpeeled) organic potato

1 oz. (a little less than ⅛ cup) sea salt

1 handful native soil and leaf litter

1 handful finely chopped wild grass (or other organic material)

1. In a medium pot over high heat, boil 2 oz. of unpeeled potato for 10 to 15 minutes until it is soft (this is your carbohydrate source, which will be used as food for microorganisms). Place the cooked potato in a mesh bag and knead into a 5-gallon container of spring- or rainwater. Add 1 oz. of sea salt (this improves mineral diversity). Take a handful of soil and leaf litter—this should contain your indigenous microorganisms—place it in a mesh bag, and blend into the water. Add a handful of finely chopped organic material, such as wild grass and pioneer plants (this should increase microbial diversity). Cover the container with cheesecloth or another breathable material to prevent debris and contaminants from entering the solution. Let sit at an ambient temperature for 72 hours.

2. After the first day, you will begin to see bubbles form on the surface of the water; this is the sign that your microorganisms have begun to multiply. Over the next day or two, the bubbles will form distinct concentric layers. After 3 days, the concentric patterns should be at their peak, signaling maximum capacity for microbial diversity and abundance. When the concentric patterns begin to dissolve or break apart, it means microbial communities are starting to die—remove the mesh bag, filter out the plant residue, and use your solution as soon as possible. The fresher the better. (It will likely take you a few tries to determine the solution's peak, but after a couple of attempts you will have a good idea of the time frame.)

3. To inoculate soil before transplanting, use enough undiluted solution to thoroughly moisten your soil—about as much as you would normally use to water your plants. (Since different soils have different capacities for water retention, a good litmus test is to pour water in little by little until the liquid starts to seep out the bottom of the pot; at that point your soil is thoroughly moistened.) When using during plant growth, you'll want to dilute the solution with water at a 1:10 ratio. You can apply this mix to the soil or as foliar spray during vegetative growth, but once your cannabis is flowering, apply only to the soil. (Store your solution in its diluted form, and as it tends to smell pretty foul, it's probably best to keep it outdoors. Note that this solution acts as a microbial starter only when used fresh, though leftover quantities still serve as a great source of nutrients.)

Facultative Anaerobic Solution

We've talked a lot about the harm anaerobic microbes can do to your soil. But like sending a thief to catch a thief, one of the best ways to combat anaerobic growth is with a specific type of bacteria known as facultative anaerobes. While they prefer to live in an anaerobic state, facultative anaerobes can also survive in an aerobic one; due to the expanded range of conditions in which they can live, they are able to outcompete almost all harmful anaerobes. And because beneficial aerobic microbes are more suited to an oxygen-rich environment, they'll outcompete the facultative anaerobes once they've done their job. This solution can be used as a successional shifter, moving compromised soil toward an aerobic state. It contains many of the same organisms that we find in ferments like kefir and—lucky for us—it's quite simple to make. Be sure to use glass, ceramic, or BPA-free plastic to ferment and store this solution.

1. Place the rice in a pint jar and fill with room-temperature water. Shake vigorously for approximately 30 minutes (feel free to take a break if your arm gets tired). The goal is to strip the rice of its starches, which will then become food for your microorganisms. Strain the liquid into a second jar, discard the rice, and allow the starchy water to ferment for 1 week. (No need to leave the jar open: the organisms you are cultivating can thrive in an anaerobic environment.) After a week, sediment layers will form at the bottom of the liquid and a film will appear across the surface—this is a sign that microbial growth has begun.

2. Take your pint of starchy liquid, add it to 1 gallon of organic milk (any kind will do—fresh or sour—as long as it does not contain artificial growth hormones, which will inhibit microbial activity) and cover it with a lid. Over the next week or two, the curds in the milk will separate from the whey. Strain the liquid and discard the curds. What is left in the whey is a community of facultative anaerobes. The smell will remind you of cheese, but should not be foul.

3. Add 1 quart of this solution and the unsulphured blackstrap molasses (which increases the diversity and abundance of the microorganisms) to your remaining water. Let it sit, covered and at room temperature, for 3 weeks, at the end of which a layer of biofilm will have formed over the top of the liquid, signaling microbial activity. Your final product should smell sweet and vinegary.

4. The base dilution rate is 5 mL per gallon of water, but you can increase the dilution without any fear of harming your plants; excess facultative anaerobes will just become food for the rest of the soil ecology. This blend can be used as a foliar spray or soil drench, and can be combined with other microbial inputs to help prevent potential anaerobic growth. It's safe to store your solution at room temperature for up to a year.

INGREDIENTS:

2 tbsp. organic brown rice

1 gallon organic milk

1 quart unsulphured blackstrap molasses

4 ½ gallons chlorine and chloramine-free water

Vegetative and Flowering Nutrient Solutions

When your cannabis plants are in vegetative and flowering growth, it's important to feed the microbial communities already present in the soil. As the microorganisms grow, they feed on organic matter and work to convert it into bioavailable plant nutrients. They'll also capture natural growth hormones, which will greatly increase the size and flowering potential of your plants. When it comes time to find your starter material, go out into the local ecosystem and find plants that are in a healthy and vigorous state of growth. (We'd encourage you to experiment with various materials, and choose different plants for each season.)

1. In a BPA-free plastic bucket or glass container, mix the chlorine- and chloramine-free water, brown sugar, and plant material (you may need to weigh down your plant material in order to keep it submerged). Cover the container with cheesecloth and let it ferment for 10 to 15 days (this process may be slightly shorter or longer depending on the season). During this period—as with the local microbiome solution—you will begin to see bubbles forming. This is a signal that you're cultivating those micro-allies.

2. At the end of 15 days, your solution should smell sweet and slightly alcoholic—if it's foul or otherwise off-putting, it may be a sign that something has gone wrong. You can now strain your liquid into another jar for storage, but fill it only to ¾ capacity, and leave it open a crack; the solution needs air to finish the work of cycling nutrients into bioavailable forms. Once the liquid ceases to bubble, you can seal it up and store it for later use. Because this solution is capturing nutrients and compounds as opposed to specific microbial communities, there is no immediate time frame in which you need to apply it—just keep in mind that after a year, it will have lost most of its nutrient content. Dilute the vegetative blend at a rate of 60 mL per gallon of water and the flowering blend at 15 mL per gallon, and apply directly to your soil or as a foliar spray.

INGREDIENTS:

Enough chlorine and chloramine-free water to fully cover your plant material

½ lb. brown sugar

1 lb. plant material

Chapter Seven

GROWING

AS WITH SO MANY ACQUIRED SKILLS, THE BEST WAY TO LEARN TO GROW CANNABIS is, simply, to grow cannabis. The pace and process will vary from plant to plant and from garden to garden, but the more crops you have under your belt, the easier it will be to experiment and adjust on the fly. Not everything is instinctual—which is why we've spent so many pages on the more technical aspects, from lighting and temperature to soil and nutrients—but we firmly believe that the more time you spend with your plants, the more intuitive the process becomes.

Cannabis needs regular care and attention, and you should plan on checking in on your plants most days. But this doesn't have to feel like a chore. For many, gardening takes on a restful, meditative quality, and there's no reason why growing cannabis should be any different. Don't stress out if your buds aren't as bountiful as you'd hoped; don't panic when problems inevitably emerge. There's a learning curve to growing, so take it all in stride.

Our goal in this chapter is to walk you through the basics of the process—from propagation all the way through flowering—and describe what kinds of growth and changes you can expect to see at each stage. We'll give you the rundown on when to adjust your controls—light, temperature, humidity, etc.—and discuss how an indoor garden can emulate cannabis's natural environments. We'll offer instructions and tips, and highlight the most common issues that arise from week to week. Just remember that growing a living thing is never a paint-by-number practice—if it were, it'd be a whole lot less interesting.

Photosynthesis, Respiration, & Transpiration

Growing cannabis doesn't require an advanced degree in botany, but there are certain principles that warrant a quick crash course. A rough understanding of a few of your plants' key processes will make the information that follows easier to digest and can go a long way when it comes to reacting to or addressing problems.

PHOTOSYNTHESIS

Photosynthesis is the process by which plants capture light energy and convert it into chemical energy. So while cannabis's fan leaves may not be good for smoking, they're doing the heavy lifting when it comes to manufacturing the plant's food. Leaves contain tiny subcellular structures called chloroplasts, which themselves contain chlorophyll—the chemical that allows plants to absorb light. That light energy reacts to carbon dioxide from the air and water from the soil to form sugars, starches, carbohydrates, and proteins; these are called photosynthates. (Oxygen is released as a byproduct.) Photosynthesis differs from species to species, but the simple equation is this: carbon dioxide + water + light energy = photosynthates and oxygen.

RESPIRATION

Once photosynthates are created, they must be metabolized. This process is called respiration. Respiration occurs in most cells and throughout the plant—in the leaves, the stems, and the roots. While photosynthesis uses carbon dioxide and water and produces oxygen and photosynthates, respiration uses oxygen and photosynthates and releases carbon dioxide and water. Essentially, energy (in the form of sugar) is "burned," allowing the plant to grow and do the internal work of living. Unlike photosynthesis—which can take place only in the light—respiration occurs in the dark as well.

TRANSPIRATION

We know that roots are pulling water from the soil—and with that water, absorbing their needed nutrients—and we know that some of that water is being used in cellular processes (about 10% is used for photosynthesis), but what happens to the rest? Almost 90% of the water that enters the plant is used for transpiration. This is the process by which moisture is carried through plants from the roots to the stomata (small, adjustable pores on the underside of each leaf), where it turns to vapor and is released into the atmosphere. Transpiration serves three essential roles: it moves minerals and sugars throughout the plant (the water serves as both a solvent and a transport); it cools the plant (much like our sweat cools our bodies); and it maintains the turgor pressure in cells, which allows them to keep their rigidity (picture the way air inflates a balloon). Several environmental factors—light, temperature, humidity, and the amount of water in the soil—can influence the rate of transpiration.

Choosing Your Plants

The most important aspect when it comes to obtaining your genetics is making sure they come from a trustworthy source—if you're spending good money, you want some assurance that you're getting what you pay for. Beyond that, there are three basic questions you need to consider when choosing your plants: What strain are you interested in cultivating? Where will you procure your genetics? Will you grow from seed or clone?

The answer to the first question will largely be determined by your preferences: what traits you're looking for, in terms of experience and flavors. Research cannabinoid levels and terpene profiles, talk to budtenders, and scour the online databases for various hybrids and phenotypes. Your options are constantly expanding. Part of the fun of growing is trying something new. But you'll also want to factor in your environment. Some strains are better suited to indoor gardens, while others thrive in outdoor settings. If you have a low ceiling in your grow room, then a landrace sativa that reaches 10 feet at maturity probably isn't your best option. If it's difficult to keep your garden entirely dark for the nighttime cycle—maybe the only room you can grow in will inevitably have people passing through at odd hours—then you might want to consider an autoflowering strain. Save yourself a headache and ask about plants that have natural resistances to pests. Remember that all cannabis plants have a distinct aroma, but some are far more potent than others. If you have housemates—or even neighbors—who don't particularly love the smell, maybe skip Chemdog, Sour Diesel, or other strains known for their overpowering odor.

If you're growing more than one varietal, be conscious of each strain's flowering time (this is especially important if you're using a single room for both vegetative and flowering growth). Once a plant is ready to flower it needs a different light cycle than it did during vegetation.

The answer to the second question might be determined by sheer availability, or it might be determined by local law. While a lot of growers are used to buying their genetics illegally online, in many parts of the country you now have the privilege of buying from seed banks, recreational shops, or dispensaries in your own community. If you have friends or colleagues who grow, don't be afraid to share, barter, or trade. (Just be sure that you're not importing their pests, fungi, or harmful bacteria.)

The answer to the third question is a bit more complicated. Seeds—standard, feminized, or autoflowering—and clones each have advantages and disadvantages. We think it's worth reading the following sections, which outline the two principal methods of propagation, before you make your first purchase.

Seeds

Growing from seed means you have a wide variety of strains to choose from and a little more flexibility in terms of your start date (as seeds can be safely stored for longer periods of time than clones). Seeds save you the risk of importing diseases, pests, fungi, or bacteria into your garden. And unlike clones, they sprout a strong taproot—the central, downward-growing root from which all the ancillary rootlets spring forth.

Remember that unless you're planning on breeding, you'll be raising only female plants. Unfortunately, you won't know whether a seed has sprouted a male or a female until 5 to 10 days into flowering, when it begins to develop preflowers. You can generally assume that half of your seeds will sprout males, which will need to be destroyed. (If you miss a male plant, you run the risk of pollinating—and likely ruining—the rest of your crop.) Germinating seeds can be a bit more involved than growing from clones, and will certainly add a couple of weeks to the process.

If you like the idea of growing from scratch, but don't want to run the risk of male infiltrators, you might consider purchasing feminized seeds, which have been specially bred to yield only female plants. This saves you the worry and headache, and gives you a more precise idea of how many plants you'll be growing. (Keep in mind that each state has different regulations on how many plants you can legally grow at one time.)

Autoflowering seeds might provide the simplest process of all. As soon as the seedlings are developed, you plant them in their final pots and turn on the lights for 18 hours per day all the way through flowering. These seeds are likewise a great option for simple outdoor grows. The downsides are that strain options are much more limited, the plants are typically lower yielding, and, if you're growing inside, your energy bills might come as a shock.

To germinate a seed is to end its hibernation, to let its stem emerge and its roots begin their development. All you really need is moisture and moderately warm temperatures, somewhere in the neighborhood of 75°F.

Our favorite germination method might be the simplest of all, as it requires no special equipment and no special nutrients: place your seeds in a glass of water,

store the glass in a warm dark place, wait 24 to 36 hours, then check for sprouts. If you see small tails emerging, you're ready to go—this is the beginning of the taproot. Some growers favor the paper-towel method: Fold a paper towel several times over, wet it with warm water, and place the seeds within its folds. Put the towel on a plate and cover it with another dish. (It's helpful to keep the seeds' environment dark and moist.) In 3 to 5 days, you should see white tails beginning to surface.

When a seed has germinated, you can transfer it to a grow medium. One of the most popular starters is a rockwool cube, which provides the seed with a proper balance of water, oxygen, and nutrients, all of which help a seedling develop its root system. Soak the rock wool for 2 hours in pH 5.5 water, place your seed—very carefully—in the cube's hole, then scratch at the rock wool until the hole is covered. (This helps to avoid exposing the seed to excess light.) Be sure to store your cubes in a humid place. In a few days, you should notice a sprout emerging from the top of the cube and the taproot from the bottom.

If you're confident in your grow medium, you can skip the rock-wool cube entirely and plant your germinated seed in a paper cup (or some other small container) of soil. But keep in mind that seedlings are especially vulnerable. Make sure that whatever growing medium you choose allows for suitable water retention—too much will foster fungus and rot, too little and you'll do permanent damage to your plants. (At this point, the plant has very little water in reserve and its root zone is still quite small.)

As soon as the seedling emerges it needs to be exposed to light for 18 to 20 hours per day—but the light should be only 20% as intense as what you'll use during vegetative growth. As you might remember from Chapter Three, light intensity falls off rapidly the farther you get from the source. So if you're using the same lamps for both stages, they should be about twice the distance now as they will be during vegetative growth.

Autoflowering seeds operate a bit differently. Their growth gets off to a much quicker start, and they don't respond well to being transplanted. Once these seeds have germinated, they should be planted directly into the same pots you'll be using until harvest. After a week or so of continuous gentle light, they can begin the cycle you'll use all the way through flowering: 18 hours on, 6 hours off.

7

Clones

As with feminized seeds, growing from clones saves you the guesswork of figuring out whether a plant is male or female. Where seeds are the result of sexual reproduction, clones are propagated asexually: a cutting is taken from a mother plant and then rooted in the soil. If you—or the person from whom you're procuring the clone—are happy with the mother, you can rest assured that the clone's genetic material will be identical. When you grow from a clone, you also shave a couple of weeks off your timeline, as you needn't germinate the seed or wait as long for the roots to develop.

You can purchase clones from a local supplier—most post their menus online—clip them yourself from your latest crop, or maintain a mother plant specifically for this purpose. It's really a question of ease and variety. If you have specific needs and preferences—if you always want to grow, say, ACDC—then continuing to use genetics you're happy with is a great idea. Medical growers and patients will often find what's most effective for them and stick closely to it. Of course, some of the pleasure of growing at home is trying a range of different strains and varietals—if that's part of your fun, don't feel bad about bypassing this process altogether.

On the downside, clones run the risk of harboring diseases, fungi, harmful bacteria, and pests. (Oftentimes, these things are in an early stage of development and very difficult to identify.) It's also possible to pass down a nutrient deficiency from an older plant to your new one. If you notice a pattern of problems from generation to generation, it might be time to start again with fresh genetics.

Clones' root systems tend to grow laterally and closer to the surface—they don't have a strong taproot like their seed-grown brethren—so if you're growing outside, they may have more trouble reaching deeper reserves of water and nutrients. (This is less of an issue for indoor gardens.) Likewise, the lack of a taproot means less of an anchor for the plant.

If you are interested in cultivating clones yourself, you'll need two separate spaces (see Chapter Four). Clones are taken during vegetative growth—whether you're collecting them from your current crop or a mother—and, until they've developed roots, must be kept under 24 hours of light in a high-humidity environment.

Many growers maintain a mother plant, which is kept in a continuous state of vegetative growth, and clip clones as needed. Just know that younger plants produce stronger offspring; if you decide to use a mother, we don't recommend letting her age more than a couple months. In our experience, it's better to take cuttings from plants that will soon go into flowering; we like to combine this task with topping (see page 120), usually in the second or third week of vegetation. This allows you to take a large healthy clone and get a replacement for the plant that will soon be leaving your vegetation room; it also minimizes the number of times you'll shock your plant (and thus stunt its growth).

TAKING AND ROOTING A CLONE

1. Choose the plant from which you'll take your clone; find a large, healthy looking node; and clip the stem 2 inches beneath it. (In a small home grow you can afford to take a nice large clone, somewhere between 3 and 6 inches tall, as it's unlikely you'll need great quantities at any one time. But they can be as small as 2 inches tall if need be.)

2. Trim away the outside tips of the leaves, keeping about half of the leaf intact. This reduces the amount of greenery the plant must keep alive and reduces crowding if you're keeping multiple clones in a single tray.

3. Dip the stem of your clone into your chosen solution. If you're using a store-bought variety, a quick dip will be fine—just leave a coating on the bottom half inch of the stem. If you're using willow water (see recipe on page 116), let your clone soak it up for 12 to 24 hours. (If you're using any kind of clone cube you'll want to soak them in a nutrient solution—such as willow water—until they're saturated.)

4. Your clone is now ready for its medium. Root or rockwool cubes have a small hole in the top center in which you'll plant the stem—just be sure it's firmly in place.

Arrange the cubes on a tray or in a container that can keep them moist and watered, and place under lights.

5. Keep humidity levels at about 80% and temperature around 78°F. (If you'd rather not keep a whole room dedicated to clone conditions, propagation domes are inexpensive and a worthwhile investment.)

6. Check on your clones daily to make sure the cubes are moist and that the plants look healthy and green. Water as needed and apply a nutrient solution once per week. In addition, spray your clones with clean water daily to keep the leaves moist.

7. After 10 days, start checking for roots. Once you notice a root ball emerging from the cube, it's time for transplanting.

Willow Water Tea

Clones need some assistance developing a strong root system. While there are plenty of synthetic rooting hormones on the market, we've had great luck with willow water. It contains natural hormones that trigger root development, and it can be used as a substitute or in combination with other organic products. You simply soak the end of your cutting for 12 to 24 hours before planting it in your starter cube or grow medium. This solution is also useful when transplanting seedlings to larger pots.

1. Gather willow leaves and young stems—the latter being more desirable—or purchase preprocessed material. (We buy ours online from Mountain Rose Herbs.) You want 1 part plant material for every 3 parts water.

2. Cut plant material into ½-inch (or smaller) pieces. The finer you process the plant material, the more thorough the extraction will be.

3. Place plant material in a large pot and fill with water, using the ratio above.

4. Bring the water to a boil and then remove from heat.

5. Cover and allow the tea to sit for 10 to 12 hours.

6. Strain the plant material. (It can be reused, but after the second extraction, you'll lose significant potency.)

7. Dilute at a rate of 60% tea to 40% water.

Vegetative Growth

The weeks between propagation and flowering are known as vegetative growth (often called "veg"). This stage is crucial in determining a plant's size and the quality of its yield—all energy goes toward making the plant taller, bulkier, and stronger. In the wild, vegetative growth happens in the spring and early summer—long days and lots of light. In the grow room, we seek to emulate (or even exaggerate) those conditions.

Whether you're working with seedlings or clones, transplanting will be determined by your space and setup. There's no reason why you can't plant a 2-inch seedling in a 5-gallon pot—the more root space, the better. (When the root system is too big for its container you'll end up with stunted growth and frail plants.) But if you're growing a larger number of plants, you can start with smaller vessels that allow you to fit more under a single light. This is friendlier toward the environment and your pocketbook. You can continue to move plants into progressively bigger containers—always making sure the entire rock-wool cube or root ball is covered in soil—but keep in mind that each transplant has the potential to stall growth for a day or two.

Once your plants are in their vegetative phase, your job is to keep them strong, healthy, and turgid. Look out for wilting and discoloration—the green should be rich and vibrant, not overly dark or yellowish. You should see significant growth every other day; if you notice a halt, you might first check the temperature—too-cold climates are often to blame. If only certain plants are struggling, and others with the same genetics are fine, it's often a local issue. Is the plant receiving enough direct light? Did it miss a watering? Remember that bugs love young plants; keep an eye out for mites and aphids.

Somewhere between 2 and 6 weeks, your plants will be ready to move into the flowering stage. The timing will depend on the strain and genetics, but also on the environment in which you're growing. The goal is to have a strong canopy that can take full advantage of the available light. If you have a greater number of plants in a smaller space, you might trigger flowering earlier; if you have only a few plants and more space to fill, they might benefit from more time in veg. Again, it varies widely, but keep in mind that at the end of vegetation, most strains will be at about 30%–50% of their eventual size.

Until you're ready to trigger that next phase of growth, we recommend the following regimen.

LIGHT CYCLE

During the first week of veg, turn your lights on for 20 hours, then off for 4. In the second week, cut back to 18 hours on, 6 hours off; keep up this cycle until you're ready to trigger flowering. Some growers opt for 24 hours of light during vegetative growth; we tend to think that's a waste of energy and creates a lot of excess heat—plants respond well to slightly cooler temperatures during

7

their night cycle. Even during vegetative growth, plants benefit from at least 4 hours of darkness, as it allows the stomata to close and reset.

TEMPERATURE AND HUMIDITY

Because vegetative growth is synonymous with summer, your plants will need a little more heat. It's best to keep the temperature right around 75°F, during both day and night cycles.

During the first week, you want to keep the humidity level slightly higher—somewhere around 75–80%. For the rest of vegetative growth, humidity should hover around 70%.

WATER

One of the best ways to judge watering needs is based on pot weight. Fill your pot with dry soil. If you have a scale handy, weigh it; if not, pick it up and feel how heavy it is. Now—before you add your plant—drench the soil until you start to see some runoff. Pick up the pot again and note the difference. Anytime the pot drops to about a quarter of the fully wet weight, it's time to water.

After the first week—once the roots have had a chance to establish themselves—don't water too often. Let the soil dry out to the touch before watering again and, when possible, do so away from the root zone; you *want* roots to extend themselves searching for water.

NUTRIENTS

If you're using liquid nutrients, make sure you have a product geared specifically toward vegetative growth. (They're usually labeled "grow" as opposed to "bloom.") If you're growing in live soil, you might add a drench of willow water tea for root development or add a mycorrhizal inoculant, which encourages the development of a mycorrhizal microbiome in your root zone. This will give your plant some help with nutrient uptake; Make sure they have nutrients available to them but aren't overloaded. (See Chapter Eight.)

One way to provide an additional dose of nutrients is a foliar feed, by which the plant absorbs a liquid solution directly through the stomata on its leaves. This can be useful as part of a regular feeding regimen, as well as when your plants need a quick dose of food to address a deficiency.

Foliar Feed

Mix ingredients in a clean container, then pour solution into a clean spray bottle—avoid anything that was previously used for chemicals—or a small garden pump sprayer. Foliar feeds can be applied up until harvest; just be aware that whatever you use on flowering plants will more than likely end up in your system when it comes time to consume your bud.

INGREDIENTS:
1 gallon water
15–30 mL seaweed extract*
15–30 mL fulvic acid*
2 tbsp. magnesium sulfate (Epsom salt)
25% of the called-for amount of your liquid fertilizer of choice (If the brand you're using calls for 1 part per 10 gallons of water, use 1 part per 40 instead.) Use "grow" products for veg and "bloom" products for flowering growth.

* Concentrations vary. Check the label for foliar dilution rate.

Canopy Management & Training

Once you have the basics down—light, temperature, humidity, airflow, water, and nutrients—and your plants are growing, the most significant thing you can do to improve your yield and the quality of your bud is to spend time getting your canopy into shape. With a few tricks and a little attention, you can make sure your plants reach their maximum potential.

Left to its own devices, cannabis will usually grow into something like a Christmas-tree shape. The leader—the plant's main shoot—receives the bulk of the energy and nutrients, and thus experiences the most growth (this is known as apical dominance). In the wild, where the movement of the sun ensures that lower portions of the plant still get light, this isn't a problem. Indoors, where your lights are stationary and positioned above your plants, a Christmas-tree shape is not the ideal figure—this is especially true if you're working with a single plant per pot.

There are numerous methods for shaping your canopy, and they differ based on whether you're working with a limited number of plants (each state has its own restrictions) or a fixed amount of space, but we tend to stick with the simplest ones. Our goals are to create wide branch structures, provide even light to as many flowering nodes as possible, and support branches as early as needed. (The less energy the plant puts into strengthening branches, the more it can put into flower production!)

LOW-STRESS TRAINING

This term refers to any canopy management technique that involves neither cutting nor pruning, but rather gradually manipulating branches to grow in whatever direction maximizes their exposure to light. Oftentimes, it's a matter of tying off individual branches so that they present themselves horizontally instead of vertically. This encourages a response called phototropism, in which a plant orients itself toward a light source. With cannabis, each individual node will reach toward the light; instead of the single cola that would have formed with a vertical branch, this method creates multiple colas. You lose that Christmas-tree shape and get something more bush-like. Low-stress training is also useful for making sure your canopy fits in your particular garden—a tent or closet with limited headroom might have different needs than a garage space with 15-foot ceilings.

When tying your branches, be sure not to use something that will harm the plant—wire and string can damage the tissue, so it's best to add a bit of padding where they touch the stems.

SUPER CROPPING

As with low-stress training, the goal of super cropping is to bend the branches until they're oriented horizontally rather than vertically. Where it differs is the tactic of strategically damaging your plants in order to trigger a stress-based response; the plant reacts as if it's being attacked, and puts additional energy into repair and growth. In the end, it's stronger for it.

To bend a mature branch without splitting or severing it, you first need to break up the cells within the branch. Find the point you want to bend and pinch it between your thumb and forefinger until you feel the rigidity of the stalk give way and it becomes malleable. You want to bend the branch without breaking the skin. Eventually, the bent point will harden and become more durable than it was previously, but in order for the branch to heal, you'll likely need to support it. You can either stake the individual branch or, if you're using trellis netting for the entire canopy, simply lay the branch across your net.

TOPPING AND TIPPING

Topping is the process of removing the terminal bud, which not only exposes lower branches to more light but also communicates that auxiliary shoots must make up for the loss of the main. Again, you end up with a flatter, bushier plant and multiple colas as opposed to a single large one.

We like to top 7 to 10 days before we trigger flowering, and then again 1 to 3 weeks later (depending on a given strain). Just make sure that you have strong growth among the lower nodes—shoots that can take advantage of their promotion. Some growers report better results topping during the night cycle, when hormones are massed at the root level—the theory is that it helps minimize the stunted growth that comes from the shock of a severed branch. When you decide the time is right, take a clean, sharp pair of shears and cut away the main shoot at a point just above the node.

Tipping is more appropriate for a denser canopy composed of smaller plants. Like topping, it allows

TIPPING

the lower branches to grow taller, receiving more light and attention, but the terminal bud remains the plant's dominant feature. The idea is to encourage each shoot to sprout two colas rather than one. It's a much smaller cut, and you want to make sure a primary pair of nodes remains. We tend to tip our plants 7 days before we trigger flowering, but—depending on the rate of growth—it can be done up to 2 weeks after.

SEA OF GREEN

While some growers play fast and loose with this term—the definition isn't entirely stable—sea of green (or SOG) generally refers to the practice of fitting a great number of plants under your lights, then instigating flowering at a relatively young age (usually after 2 or 3 weeks of veg). Remember that plants grown outdoors spend an entire spring and summer in vegetative growth, while indoor plants can make the switch whenever the grower decides the time is right. If you have no limit on the number of plants you can grow—and procuring the seeds or clones isn't an issue—the sea of green method can be a highly efficient use of space and time. It means less volume per plant, but constant turnover. (If you're not interested in growing continuously, stick with a longer veg cycle, get more yield from each harvest, and then take some time off to enjoy the fruits of your labor.) If you have limited space or limited time, SOG might be right for you.

Keep in mind that without the benefit of a longer period of vegetative growth, many sativa-dominant strains will still need to be staked or netted to support their weight. Most indica strains, if flowering when they're around 6–12 inches tall, will not need much support.

7

Sexing

If you're growing from nonfeminized seedlings, it's absolutely crucial to identify and separate—this usually means destroy—male plants. If you allow a male to bloom, it will pollinate your females, which will divert their energy to producing seeds instead of developing buds. While there are some early signs—male plants tend to grow taller and thinner, and some strains form early preflowers right at the node between the stem and leaf—none of these traits are consistent enough to rely on.

To know for sure what you're dealing with, you have to flower the seedlings. This is done by briefly introducing them to a flowering cycle, then—once males are purged—returning the females to vegetative growth conditions. During the first week, use a light regimen of 12 hours on and 12 hours off. Observe the plants closely every day and look for small pollen sacs; males sprout ball-shaped flowers (1) whereas females sprout hairlike pistils (2). (Males typically flower quicker than females.) Once they show the telltale signs, remove the males and reinstate the longer light cycle.

Unsurprisingly, this detour into flowering can be disruptive to vegetative growth. Another option—if you're working with more than one grow space—is to take a cutting of each plant, place that cutting in a glass of water or a rock-wool cube, then apply a 12-hour light cycle to the clones. Your main plants will remain in veg while your cuttings reveal themselves. (Just be sure that each plant is correctly identified with its corresponding clone.)

One thing to keep in mind: if you are flowering multiple plants in a single pot and counting on the initial planting pattern to fill your canopy, you will have a problem once you separate the males. Consider growing a single plant per pot, arranging them in a denser pattern before sexing, then spreading them out after you rid your garden of males.

①

②

Flowering Growth

As days get shorter and nights get cooler, cannabis plants stop focusing on their growth and begin to direct their energy toward reproduction. In the wild, this happens naturally with the change of seasons. In the grow room, it's a deliberate decision. If you've successfully purged your garden of male plants, of course, reproduction won't be in the cards. Luckily, the resinous buds that female plants count on to carry on the family name (and genetic lineage) are exactly what you'll be looking for when it comes time to harvest.

Whether you're moving plants from a vegetative room to a flowering room or keeping them in place—and altering the light, temperature, and humidity levels—the flip from veg to flower can come as a shock; the healthier the plants, the easier time they have adjusting. (All the more reason to take good care of them during vegetative growth.)

FLOWERING: WEEK ONE

Right after the flip to flowering, vegetative growth accelerates; vertical growth remains steady and lateral growth takes off, with nodes along the main stalk developing into real branches. This is typically when plants start to flower, but if those clusters aren't apparent right from the outset, don't panic—there is plenty of variation at this stage.

- Set your lights to a cycle of 12 hours on, 12 hours off. This will be the schedule from now until harvest.

- The temperature around the canopy should be about 77°F when the lights are on and 68°F when they're off. These settings can remain the same all the way through the end of week six.

- Lower the humidity level to 65%.

- Examine your canopy for holes. Which branches and nodes might fill them? Now is the time to start training your plants (see pages 119–121 for instructions) and filling the gaps to create a full, even canopy.

- Water regularly, but don't overdo it. It's okay if the deeper reaches remain moist, but make sure the surface of your soil has a chance to dry. (Continue to use the water-weight test we discussed on page 118.)

- Since nitrogen consumption is approaching a peak, deficiency can be a danger; this is true whether you're using liquid nutrients or a living-soil method. (See page 132 for further signs and symptoms and tips on how to introduce nitrogen into your soil.)

- Excess light is often a problem if you've transported your plants from a separate vegetative room. If your leaves are showing signs of burn, you may need to dim or raise your lights (see page 130).

- If there's no sign of flowering by the end of the week, check your light timer to confirm you're giving your plants a full night cycle, and make sure that your room is sufficiently dark—with the lights off, you shouldn't be able to see the canopy clearly. Check the room's temperature at the coldest part of the night; if it dips below 60°F, you should supplement some heat.

WEEK TWO

The second week is when flower clusters really start to show themselves. You should be seeing groups of pistils emerging from the nodes, topped by small stigmas. By the end of this week, your plants may well be twice as tall and wide as they were at the end of veg. (Of course, growth rate varies based on strain and genetics.)

- Lower the humidity level to 60%.

- Continue to shape your canopy by pruning, training, and super cropping; ideally, every square inch of area under the light will be covered with nodes and leaves. (And nodes should be spaced out as evenly as is achievable.)

- Make sure to keep your soil well watered. Respiration is high this week, thus water uptake should increase.

- As your canopy gets denser, airflow becomes increasingly important. Make sure your fans and ventilation are providing adequate circulation.

- Toward the end of the week, you will likely need to clear leaves away from the nodes. When cleaning your canopy, keep in mind that every leaf has a fixed number of stomata on its underside; as the leaf grows, these stomata spread out but don't increase. A newer, smaller leaf has the same capacity to respire as an older, bigger one, so it's fine to clear the latter first.

- Calcium and magnesium are in high demand, so deficiency can be a problem. Supplement as needed. (See pages 133–134.)

- If your plants haven't shown substantial growth this week, there's almost certainly something wrong in your garden. Check your light, temperature, and humidity settings, and look for signs of water and nutrient deficiency.

WEEK THREE

In the third week, vertical growth begins to slow, but shooting from the stalk accelerates; this is your plants making room for flowers between the nodes. Healthy white pistils should be in abundance, and behind them, calyxes will start to become apparent. This is the stage when you will notice definite flower sets; their positions on the nodes determine where buds will form along the branches.

- Continue to shape your canopy to ensure an even profile; this is a good opportunity for low-stress training.

- Not much canopy cleaning should be needed, but feel free to prune the occasional leaf if it's blocking a neighboring plant from getting sufficient light.

- Your plants are absorbing quite a bit of water this week, so be sure to check the soil daily to make sure they're getting what they need.

- Monitor the airflow to ensure sufficient circulation.

- As your plants form new stems, they need plenty of food. If you're using compost, now would be a good time for top-dressing. If you're using liquid nutrients, make sure they're in good supply.

COMMON ISSUES

- In terms of bud formation, the density now is more or less what you'll end up with. Heavy leaf growth will continue and buds will develop, but you won't see substantially more flower sites. If there are fewer than expected, take a note for next time. You might need to veg longer, prune and train differently (or earlier), or just plant more seedlings. Some trial and error is natural. Don't fret!

- If you notice your plants' pistils are browning or look otherwise unhealthy, it's a good indication you have a problem. Try to rule out environmental stress and physical damage; too much handling and brushing roughly against the pistils will often cause harm. If you're relatively certain this isn't the case, you're likely looking at a nutrient or pest problem. (See Chapter Eight for further signs.)

WEEK FOUR

The fourth week is typically the end of vertical and lateral stretching. Your plants are ensuring that nodes along the branches gain access to even light. Your flowers are putting on weight and the foliage is becoming increasingly dense. Most of the plant should be solid green in color, but flower formation points and new growth will take on a slightly lighter shade.

TASKS

- Lower the humidity level to 55%.

- Your goal at this point should be a flat canopy and uniformity of flower sites. Continue to train your plants, filling in any gaps in coverage—soon the branches will be too rigid.

- Remove excess foliage, starting with older leaves that are blocking flower sites from receiving adequate light.

- Water consumption will start to dip this week; while you still want to keep an eye on the soil daily, be careful not to overwater.

COMMON ISSUES

- If you see uneven or simply not enough light in the canopy, now would be a good time to pull excess leaves.

- Overwatering will result in less turgid leaves, but if you notice clawing—a curling of the leaves' tips—this is usually due to nitrogen excess. (See page 132.)

- Phosphorus consumption is peaking this week, so if you see signs of deficiency, you may need to supplement what's available in the soil. (See page 132.)

FLOWERING: WEEK FIVE

The fifth week is usually the make-or-break point for bud structure. Flowers are stacking, swelling, and forming sets—you should see calyxes assembling along the bud stems. You should also start to see crystal-white formations across the surface of the buds—this is the visible beginning of trichome development.

TASKS

- Check your stalks and stems to make sure they're well supported. As buds grow heavier, many strains need help standing upright; you can stake individual branches or use a trellis net (available at most gardening stores) to create a grid that will help keep your whole crop erect.

- Make sure the temperature, airflow, and humidity are in check. Now is the time when environmental problems can wreak havoc on a crop if something is too far out of balance; daily attention is needed.

- Prune any small branches that aren't getting enough light (and thus won't be able to form desirable flowers). These will only draw energy away from the buds you'll soon harvest.

- Water soil and perform foliar applications as needed.

COMMON ISSUES

- If bud structures look loose, overly airy, or otherwise undesirable, you'll need to go through the checklist of possible problems. Are there signs of excess nitrogen? Have you been overwatering (or watering too late in the day)? Is there insufficient light?

- Depending on when your plants' phosphorous consumption peaks, deficiency or excess could be an issue. Continue to keep an eye out for symptoms. (See page 132.)

- Now's the time to be diligent in checking for bud rot. Using your jeweler's loupe, regularly inspect your flowers for a whitish-gray film. (Continue this diligence until harvest.)

WEEK SIX

In the sixth week, stacked calyxes are beginning to swell and close into buds. You've probably started to notice that familiar cannabis smell.

TASKS

- Lower the humidity level to 50%.

- Pruning is no longer necessary, but remove older fan leaves—anything yellow or wilted—as needed (particularly if they're blocking light or airflow).

- Water consumption usually spikes again around this point; you should still let the surface dry out, but water deeply and allow for consistent moisture below.

COMMON ISSUES

- Your plants are absorbing peak levels of potassium this week, so keep an eye out for signs of deficiency and supplement as needed. (See page 133.)

- Pests love weak and dying plant material; removing older leaves—and inspecting your garden for eggs, larvae, and insects—will help prevent an outbreak.

WEEK SEVEN

In the seventh week, buds are continuing to swell, as are the trichomes, which should now look like symmetrical, upright mushrooms. Energy is being diverted to essential oil production, and unless you have a longer-flowering strain, you can expect pistils to start to take on an orange or red color. (Soon, they'll shrivel and die.) The mild aroma you may have smelled during the past couple of weeks is likely much more apparent.

TASKS

- Try to keep the temperature of your leaves below 72°F. (An infrared heat gun is a useful, inexpensive tool for checking this.) Reducing heat will preserve essential oils and signal to your plant that rather than focusing on bud growth, it should expend its energy on oil and resin production. If possible, dim the output of your lights (if not, you might try raising them slightly to decrease direct heat).

- Lower the humidity level to 45%.

- Continue to supply your plants with potassium, as it's necessary for oil production.

COMMON ISSUES

- If you see trichome development issues—such as small or nonexistent heads—look to environmental stress, physical damage, and finally potassium or phosphorous deficiency/excess.

- High temperatures and too much light can cause burning and hamper oil production. (See page 130 for further signs and symptoms.)

WEEK EIGHT & BEYOND

In the eighth week, your plants are nearing the end of their reproductive cycle; buds are giving their last swell and pistils are continuing to die. That cannabis aroma is at its peak, buds are swollen, and trichomes are full of resin. If you notice some leaf discoloration, don't panic: it's normal.

TASKS

- Using a jeweler's loupe, check the ripeness of your trichomes to determine when it's time to harvest. (See Chapter Nine for further discussion.)

- Clear dead or dying leaves from your canopy.

- Keep a close eye on the temperature, making sure it stays in the low 70s when the lights are on. Anything warmer and you'll risk losing essential oils.

- At this point, you should no longer add nutrients to your water. There is some debate around this "flushing process" in the organic growing community. Since you aren't using synthetic fertilizers, you probably don't need to rid your soil of the excess salt and metals they cause to accumulate. But regardless, it's unnecessary to keep adding nutrients when your plants are this far along.

COMMON ISSUES

- In dark, humid spaces—especially those filled with ripe buds and dying leaves—mold becomes a great danger. Try to keep your humidity level as close to 40% as possible, particularly when the lights are off.

Chapter Eight

TROUBLESHOOTING

WHEN IT COMES TO SOLVING YOUR GARDEN'S PROBLEMS, THE BEST OFFENSE is a good defense. By now you've read our suggestions and—with any luck—your plants are benefiting from proper airflow and humidity, from ideal temperature and lighting, and from a healthy diet of water and nutrients (aided, we hope, by thriving communities of microscopic allies).

Still, cannabis is a living, breathing thing, and growing it—at least outside a sterile lab environment—is bound to be a variable process. You'll rarely get *everything* right, and when your crop throws you a curveball, you'll need to respond. This chapter aims not only to outline some best practices in terms of prevention, but also to help you identify what ails your plants, and offer some advice and prescriptions for problems that may arise.

The best thing you can do is stay attentive. Take time to check in on your garden. Don't just hastily look your plants up and down to see how they've grown—flip over the leaves, inspect the base, break out your jeweler's loupe. See any minuscule eggs? Unhealthy yellowing? Is something moving?! If anything looks out of the ordinary, act fast. Infestations—be they insects or mold—tend to spread quickly. Nutrient deficiencies are harder to rebound from the longer they go untreated. The damage from light leaks will only get worse with time.

One thing we won't encourage you to do—no matter how tempting it might be at that critical moment—is to spray your plants with pesticides. Not only is it harmful to your cannabis and your soil, it's also dangerous for whoever inhales or ingests the flower.

Light Problems

LIGHT LEAKS

If you've made it this far, you know that maintaining distinct light cycles is crucial, especially when it comes time for flowering. A light leak during your nighttime cycle can cause real problems. Each strain reacts differently—some are particularly sensitive, some have a high tolerance, and autoflowering varieties are entirely immune. But errant light confuses most plants, causing unusual growth—stretching of the leaves and stem as well as abnormal flower formations. The stress will often cause a delay in flowering. If you notice light coming through, the solution is simple: cover any crack or gap where it gets in.

But if a light leak is prolonged or powerful enough, you might see a more dramatic outcome: a female plant, feeling that her future generations are under threat, will become hermaphroditic. Depending on the size of your crop, it might be wisest to remove the compromised plant from the garden, lest you run the risk of pollinating the rest.

LIGHT BURN

Even during your daytime cycle, there's such a thing as too much light. If your plants' leaves start to take on a brown or yellow tint around the edges while the veins remain green, there's a good chance you're dealing with light burn. This generally means that your light setup is too close to your plants. (Remember: proper distance varies depending on the type of bulb you're using.) Light burn can lead to dramatically reduced yields and less potent buds, since the damaged leaves can no longer effectively take in the energy plants need to produce and develop flowers.

If you're unable to raise your lights, your best bet is to bend and train your plants so that they're below the threshold of the danger zone.

Many beginning gardeners mistake light burn for a nutrient deficiency—the discoloration can look quite similar. The location of the discoloration is the biggest giveaway. Most nutrient deficiencies affect the lower, older parts of the plant. Light burn will always be concentrated at the top of the plant, closest to the lights.

Nutrient Deficiencies & Excesses

Whether you're taking the living-soil approach or feeding your plants' liquid nutrients, a well-balanced diet will ensure vigorous growth and the best-quality buds. Nourished plants are less susceptible to fungus and disease—taking care of them on the front end will save you a headache later.

In a perfect world, your cannabis would have a carefully calibrated equilibrium of more than 20 nutrients, and just the right amount of water to deliver them. Spoiler: you'll probably never achieve that platonic ideal. But that doesn't excuse you from monitoring your plants' nutrient intake and finding balance where you can. There are a number of soluble nutrients that can greatly improve your plants' health and yields, but the Big Three that most growers concern themselves with are nitrogen, phosphorous, and potassium: N-P-K. In this section, we'll walk you through these and others, with an eye on how to treat deficiencies and excesses.

(**1**) Nitrogen deficiency (**2**) Potassium deficiency

8

NITROGEN (N)

Nitrogen is a mobile macroelement, one of the most important in terms of plant and leaf growth during the vegetative stage. It's key for the production of chlorophyll—and thus your plants' ability to photosynthesize—and it's essential for tissue production.

DEFICIENCY

Nitrogen deficiency is one of the most common cannabis ailments, particularly in the first week of flowering and again toward the end. It usually shows up as a general chlorosis (diseased yellowing) of the older leaves, starting at the edges and making its way inward. Newer leaves won't grow to their full size, and eventually you'll see a red discoloration of the stem. Without large, vibrant leaves your plants lose the ability to create energy, which stifles flower production (and hence lowers your yields).

OUR RECOMMENDATION

Blood meal, guano, and cottonseed meal are all high in easily soluble nitrogen. Deficient plants usually recover relatively quickly—a week or so after the above nutrients are added.

EXCESS

When your plants get too much nitrogen, they will often take on a dull, dark green color; the leaves will curl under and turn clawlike. The main stalk often becomes brittle and inflexible, which leads to breakage. Excess nitrogen also makes your plants more vulnerable to pests and disease.

OUR RECOMMENDATION

Removing nitrogen can be a slow and difficult process, but laying mulch—such as sawdust—on top of your soil can draw some of the excess nutrient away from your root zone. (You can also add leaves and other high-carbon materials to the mix.) For a severe problem, this is typically too slow a process, in which case you'll likely have to flush your grow medium with water, using a 3-to-1 water-to-soil ratio. Once your medium is flushed, reintroduce nutrients using half doses until your levels are normalized (at which point, you can carry on as usual).

PHOSPHORUS (P)

Phosphorus is likewise a mobile macroelement, but its major achievement is stimulating root mass and flower sets—it's important throughout the life of the plant, but critical during early rooting stages and flower production. It provides energy to the plant and directly participates in its metabolism.

DEFICIENCY

Phosphorus deficiency is less common, but when it does occur, it's typically in the fourth or fifth week of flowering, when consumption is high. At extreme levels, a shortage of phosphorus can be fairly damaging. You'll first notice purple splotches on yellowing leaves and dark purple coloring of the petioles. (Keep in mind that some strains have natural purple hues.) As the deficiency progresses, plants will feel woody and start to show symptoms of chlorosis, with more and more leaves turning yellow. If the deficiency remains untreated, you can count on massive defoliation and—eventually—death.

OUR RECOMMENDATION

Greensand, rock phosphate, manure, and guano are all rich in phosphorous and can be added directly to your soil.

EXCESS

Phosphorus excess typically results in a massive lockout of other elements, such as calcium, copper, iron, magnesium, and zinc. It's difficult to identify, but you should look for yellow or white coloring between the veins.

OUR RECOMMENDATION

For a severe problem, flush your grow medium with water, using a 3-to-1 water-to-soil ratio. Once your medium is flushed, reintroduce nutrients using half doses until your levels are normalized (at which point, you can carry on as usual).

POTASSIUM (K)

Potassium is the Swiss Army knife of mobile macroelements—it's found throughout the plant and is crucial in all stages of growth and bud development. It synthesizes carbohydrates, proteins, and amino acids, and, together with phosphorus, it improves the strength and resilience of the root system. Potassium also aids in the conveyance of water and in protecting the plant from disease, harmful bacteria, and mold.

DEFICIENCY

Considering its heavy workload, you can imagine that a lack of potassium has damaging effects. Minor deficiencies are harder to observe at first glance—plants lacking in this nutrient often grow slightly taller than their potassium-rich peers—but if you look closely, there's usually browning or yellowing along the edges of older leaves. At more extreme levels, you can expect stunted growth, chlorotic spotting, and red discoloration on the leaves and stems. Keep an eye out in the sixth week of flowering, when your plants' potassium consumption is at its peak.

OUR RECOMMENDATION

Adding wood ash and liquefied kelp to your soil can boost potassium levels. Don't expect affected leaves to recover, but you should be able stave off further damage.

EXCESS

Potassium excess affects the plant by blocking the absorption of other elements such as calcium, magnesium, zinc, and iron. The best indicator is a white or very light yellow coloring between the leaves' veins.

OUR RECOMMENDATION

For a severe problem, flush your grow medium with water, using a 3-to-1 water-to-soil ratio. Once your medium is flushed, reintroduce nutrients using half doses until your levels are normalized (at which point, you can carry on as usual).

CALCIUM (Ca)

Calcium is an immobile secondary element—once it is locked in the plant tissue, it doesn't travel to other parts of the plant. Anything that interrupts the movement of water can cause a calcium deficiency. (For example, if relative humidity is too high, your plants will transpire less water and calcium may not be distributed to all of the plants' cells.) Calcium plays a vital role in root development, the strength of cell walls, and protein synthesis. It lends support to other elements that, when combined, participate in various metabolic processes (such as the creation of vitamins).

DEFICIENCY

Calcium deficiencies can lead to weak branches and stems, leaf necrosis, and improper development of the root system. All of these eventually mean stunted growth and small yields. Early symptoms will show up in the youngest leaves, which turn very dark green before developing brown and yellow spots. As new shoots emerge, they look shrunken and disfigured.

OUR RECOMMENDATION

The easiest way to supplement calcium deficiencies in your soil is with slaked lime (or calcium hydroxide), which can be added—in very small doses—to your watering regimen.

EXCESS

When your cannabis plant has too much calcium it will often block out other essential nutrients, such as potassium, magnesium, and iron. Early on, if calcium levels are extremely high, you may see stunted growth.

OUR RECOMMENDATION

For a severe problem, flush your grow medium with water, using a 3-to-1 water-to-soil ratio. Once your medium is flushed, reintroduce nutrients using half doses until your levels are normalized (at which point, you can carry on as usual).

MAGNESIUM (Mg)

A mobile secondary element, magnesium moves around the plant as needed—from older leaves to new ones. As a central element of chlorophyll, it's essential for photosynthesis and critical to a plant's ability to take advantage of nutrients and to create sugars and carbohydrates.

DEFICIENCY

Magnesium deficiency starts with the lower leaves, then gradually spreads to the rest of the plant. While it's difficult to detect early on, the first signs typically appear in the tips of the leaves, which turn brown and curl up. Brown spots and yellowing patterns increase in number and size, and you'll eventually see some discoloration in the veins. Minor deficits won't cause too much damage, but you can expect a decrease in the number and size of buds.

OUR RECOMMENDATION

You can easily increase magnesium in your soil by adding Epsom salt or dolomitic limestone to your watering regimen. Epsom salt can be used as a foliar application as well (the latter tends to be a quicker cure).

EXCESS

Magnesium excess is rare in cannabis, and difficult to identify, but if you do find yourself with staggering quantities, it will cause a barrier to calcium absorption.

OUR RECOMMENDATION

For a severe problem, flush your grow medium with water, using a 3-to-1 water-to-soil ratio. Once your medium is flushed, reintroduce nutrients using half doses until your levels are normalized (at which point, you can carry on as usual).

SULFUR (S)

Sulfur is crucial to root growth, vegetative growth, and protein synthesis, but it also contributes to cannabis's aromas and flavors.

DEFICIENCY

Sulfur deficiency is rare, but when it does occur, you can expect plant growth to slow, stems to become woody, and leaves to yellow starting from the base and moving out to the tips.

OUR RECOMMENDATION

Epsom salt, added to your watering regimen or as a foliar application, is a sure way to introduce additional sulfur. Keep in mind that sulfur moves very slowly through plants, so any sort of deficiency or excess remedy requires patience; it'll most likely take several days before you start to see an improvement.

EXCESS

At extreme levels, too much sulfur will lead to stunted leaf and bud development.

OUR RECOMMENDATION

For a severe problem, flush your grow medium with water, using a 3-to-1 water-to-soil ratio. Once your medium is flushed, reintroduce nutrients using half doses until your levels are normalized (at which point, you can carry on as usual).

Integrated Pest Management

The term integrated pest management (IPM) refers to a multifaceted approach to dealing with pests—not just insects or rodents, but fungus, bacteria, and other harmful pathogens. An IPM strategy is something normally reserved for commercial farms, but we've found that the same principles apply to a home grow. Still, if you're going to have success with this method, there are a few things to keep in mind—particularly at the scale we're discussing in this book.

FIRST: incorporate good practices. The idea is to minimize the risk and potential success of a pest. This typically means remaining diligent about cleanliness and environmental factors on an ongoing basis.

SECOND: define "pest" (at least in relation to your plants). While this may seem like a simple task, it can be a bit deceiving. A pest is an organism—insect, fungi, bacteria, etc.—that conflicts with the success of your garden. A small infestation of crane flies may look alarming, but it'll do no harm—they don't eat cannabis. When it comes to live soil, especially, many beneficial organisms will be present. (Luckily, most of them are microscopic.) Save your energy—and sleepless nights—for pests that warrant it.

THIRD: this is management, not annihilation. You're trying to control the effect of pests, but this doesn't inherently mean you must eradicate them. It's about discerning the level of impact a pest is having, and deciding what level of control is appropriate. To put it simply, if it costs more to treat the problem than the problem itself will cost, maybe the issue isn't worth addressing. In a business, this is an easy formula—it's purely dollars and cents. In a home grow, the answer may be more subjective, but the principle remains. We can't control everything, and it isn't practical to try.

With those assumptions in mind, we'll break down the three basic categories of IPM—physical controls (also called "cultural" or "natural" controls), biological controls, and chemical controls. We'll then walk through a few of the most common and damaging grow room pests, give you tips to identify what you're dealing with, and offer suggestions as to how it might be treated—physically, biologically, and chemically.

8

PHYSICAL CONTROLS

This strategy is about making your garden uninhabitable for whatever you're doing battle with. If you can successfully identify a pest, you can make the environment undesirable to it. If you're dealing with insects that lay their eggs in the soil, it might be prudent to add companion plants to your pots, such as clover, which will block the insects' access. If you've got something that thrives in wet conditions—say, a fungus gnat—you might control the population by letting your topsoil dry out.

BIOLOGICAL CONTROLS

Our next strategy uses natural enemies of your pest—biopesticides and predators—to reduce or eliminate their population. In the case of cannabis, these include pathogens (bacteria, fungi, and other microorganisms) and insects. Biological controls are effective only when they are targeted toward the correct pest—a predatory mite that eats aphids will likely have no effect on a spider mite—so again, it's important to correctly diagnose the issue if you hope to treat it.

CHEMICAL CONTROLS

We're not talking harmful chemicals (you may be getting sick of hearing us say it: toxic pesticides should be avoided at all costs), but if you've already tried to fix your environment and introduce the latest biological controls, a nonsynthetic chemical spray can be a useful last resort, and there's no shame in using one if the other methods fail. Chemical controls can help you get things back in shape and in a manageable condition. Again, selecting the right tool for the right pest is key; a fungicide, for instance, will do little to fight mites.

FUNGUS GNATS

Fungus gnats are small, delicate flying insects (sometimes mistaken for mosquitoes) that favor laying their eggs in soil. When those eggs hatch, the larvae feed on the soil's organic matter—in particular, your plants' roots. If that's not bad enough, they have a tendency to spread other harmful pests—notably russet mites—bacteria, and diseases. The damage these gnats do to a plant's roots can also make way for fungus problems.

Keep an eye out for fungus gnat larvae around the base of your plants (they're very small and translucent, so some magnification will come in handy). You'll likely first notice full-grown fungus gnats flying around your grow room. This is the time to act; don't wait until your plants begin to show symptoms. Sticky traps are a good way to keep an eye out for flying insects, and a good way to monitor whether or not your attempts at remediation are working.

PHYSICAL CONTROLS

Don't water as often; fungus gnats thrive in wet conditions. Allow the surface of your soil to become completely dry for 24 hours before watering again. Plant cover crops—such as clover—in the pot alongside your cannabis. This will prevent the fungus gnat from accessing the soil to lay eggs. Use screens on any open windows or ventilation, and place yellow sticky traps near your canopy to trap adult gnats during their mating period.

BIOLOGICAL CONTROLS

Bacillus thuringiensis—available in most gardening stores as a product called BTI—is an effective bacterium to combat fungus gnat larvae. It can be applied either as a topdressing for your soil (when sprinkled on top, it will time-release each time you water) or in a liquid form that can be added during watering. If BTI doesn't work on its own, try using beneficial nematodes in conjunction with your applications. These microscopic, nonsegmented, wormlike critters are parasitic to insect pests—they burrow inside fungus gnats and kill them. They must be obtained fresh—they come in a sealed pouch of granular mix you add to your watering—and unless you have a very well-stocked gardening shop nearby, you'll probably need to order them online.

CHEMICAL CONTROLS

Any good natural gardening store will sell you a specially formulated blend of essential oils—often rosemary and clove oil—made specifically for soilborne pests. Just add these to your watering regimen as instructed (and worry not: these blends are safe, effective, and pleasant to use).

SPIDER MITES

Unfortunately, spider mites are common in cannabis gardens, and once they arrive, they're quick to reproduce. They typically reside on the undersides of leaves and around the buds, feeding on the individual cells and thus robbing your plants of nutrients. They protect their tiny, translucent eggs with silk webbing. Spider mites are so small that they often go unnoticed until it's too late, but if an infestation is significant, it can raze an entire plant overnight. Keep an eye out for speckles of yellow, orange, or brown; these signs are often wrongly diagnosed as nutrient deficiencies, but if you notice discoloration, grab your jeweler's loupe and check under your leaves for mites and eggs.

PHYSICAL CONTROLS

Spider mites spread very easily: via your clothing, your person, your pets, you name it. Be especially careful of tracking them into or out of other growers' spaces. They can also enter your space through the ventilation; if this becomes a regular problem, consider installing a fine-dust filter. Since spider mites prefer dry climates, upping your humidity levels during vegetative growth can help deter reproduction.

BIOLOGICAL CONTROLS

If your infestation is on the smaller side, predatory mites are an effective and fairly inexpensive option. You can introduce them to your garden regularly as a precautionary measure; they will eat spider-mite eggs that do show up, and help prevent a full-fledged invasion.

CHEMICAL CONTROLS

A weekly foliar application of neem oil—pressed from the nuts of the Indian neem tree—is an excellent preventative solution. (You'll want to focus primarily on the undersides of the leaves.) Cinnamon-clove tea, when added to your watering regimen, can also be used as a precaution. But if you're in need of a curative—or if your friends have spider mites and you're worried you may have tracked them into your grow room—you should switch to AzaMax, an antifeedant and insect-growth regulator made from azadirachtin. (In this case, it's best to use as a foliar application, but AzaMax can be used as a soil drench as well.) If eggs are detected, increase your application to once every 3 days, then continue applying weekly once the problem has subsided.

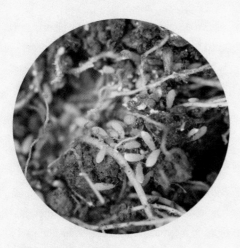

ROOT APHIDS

Also known as grape phylloxera, root aphids have long been the bane of wine makers and can quickly become a headache for cannabis growers as well. These tiny insects feed on leaves and roots, which swell and harden due to a sappy enzyme the aphids leave behind. This cuts off the flow of water and nutrients and opens the door for harmful fungi and diseases. Eventually root aphids will stunt a plant's growth and diminish your yields.

Unfortunately, the best way to recognize the problem is underneath the surface of your soil. These insects assemble around roots and form a waxy, white coating—but you may not know to look until you see your plants suffering.

PHYSICAL CONTROLS

We recommend hanging yellow sticky traps near your ventilation source and checking them regularly to see if winged aphids (or other pests) have made their way into your grow room. You should also be careful about where you buy your soil and clones. Many large-scale commercial growers and nurseries struggle with these and other pests; it's always a good idea to ask questions and read reviews.

BIOLOGICAL CONTROLS

Beauveria bassiana is a living fungus used in the insecticide BotaniGard. In theory, it can kill off both adults and larvae, but it's probably better used in combination with a chemical control. Once those applications have taken hold, beneficial nematodes (see our section on fungus gnats) can be effective in getting rid of any remaining larvae, ensuring the aphids don't return.

CHEMICAL CONTROLS

Diatomaceous earth—a siliceous sedimentary rock—can act as a safe natural pesticide. The root aphids absorb the powder, which dries them out. Topdress your soil with a light uniform layer, water, and allow it to dissolve. You can reapply as needed, for as long as the aphids remain. Pyrethrin is effective as well. Apply it as a root drench during watering, but know your combative application rate will be determined by the brand you choose. (Follow the manufacturer's instructions.)

POWDERY MILDEW

This fungal disease is easy to recognize: it starts with small dark specks on the tops of your leaves, but as the fungus takes hold, you start to see a dusting that looks like white powder. Unfortunately, those first signs aren't apparent until a week after the initial infection. Your plants' development will slow, their leaves will yellow, and eventually they'll whither. Because mildew spores can remain dormant until they find the right host and environment, they can easily be introduced by infected cuttings or simply because they've been tracked in from an infected garden. (Roses and hops, we should warn you, are frequent accomplices.)

PHYSICAL CONTROLS

Good air circulation is the best way to prevent powdery mildew from settling in your garden; this means making sure you're getting sufficient airflow into and out of your room, and that your canopy isn't overcrowded. Keeping your space clean and making sure you don't have excess moisture will go a long way. While certain biopesticides need to be applied at night, it's usually better to apply foliar sprays when your lights are on—wet leaves in a warm, dark room are asking for trouble. If you do notice mildew, carefully wash and dry your plants; this won't cure the root problem, but it can keep symptoms from spreading.

BIOLOGICAL CONTROLS

Bacillus subtilis, a bacterium found in our gastrointestinal tracts, is useful both as a preventative and a combative measure. Serenade makes a popular spray-bottle version. (As it's useful against several types of fungal problems, we recommend keeping a bottle around.) *Ampelomyces quisqualis* is a beneficial hyperparasite and will likewise slow the growth of powdery mildew. (The common brand name is AQ10.)

CHEMICAL CONTROLS

Neem oil—in addition to its insect-control benefits—is effective as an antifungal agent, especially when used as a foliar spray. (There are many different products out there, so use as directed.) AzaMax is an excellent precautionary step as well.

GRAY MOLD (AKA BUD ROT)

Botrytis cinerea—which oenophiles will recognize as the noble rot sometimes used to make sweet dessert wines—is among the most common fungal problem for cannabis growers. In the wine world, it can be a benefit, removing water from grapes and leaving behind more concentrated sugars. In your grow room, not so much. You'll first notice it in the buds—a whitish-gray film that grows fuzzy as it worsens—but eventually it spreads to leaves and stems. Depending on the humidity levels, it can create a slimy substance or dry out the plant material completely, leaving it to crumble. Spores are airborne and can be transported through open ventilation, or they can ride your coattails from an infected garden.

PHYSICAL CONTROLS

Keep your humidity levels down, your air circulation high, and water only when your lights are on. Use clean, sharp tools for pruning and manicuring, as gray mold has an easier time infecting damaged plants. If you do notice bud rot, carefully cut away the affected buds and dispose of them in an airtight vessel outside of your home (and be sure to sanitize your hands and tools immediately). At this point, your number one goal is to prevent further contamination.

BIOLOGICAL CONTROLS

Regular applications of *Bacillus subtilis*—under the brand name Serenade—will help your plants stave off a mold outbreak. It's not a bad idea to start weekly foliar applications in the third week of flowering.

CHEMICAL CONTROLS

Once again, neem oil is effective at preventing bud rot, both from forming and from spreading.

8

Chapter Nine

THE HARVEST:
DRYING, TRIMMING, & CURING

SO YOU'VE PUT IN THE TIME. YOU'VE RAISED YOUR SEEDS OR CLONES AS IF THEY were your own children: you've fed them, you've watered them, you've cared for them—you watched as they sprouted into full-grown plants (and proudly showed pictures of their progress to your friends). But before you lie back and let your plants take care of you, there are a few final steps: drying, trimming, and curing.

As with all of the big cannabis cultivation questions, you'll hear self-righteous hard-liners preaching a One True Way. This sort of prescriptive, high-and-mighty attitude is common in the industry, and we want to reiterate that there is no *one* right way to grow your own. There *are* some critical components that you should be wary of deviating from, but these methods are primarily tied to work flow, space, and how you want to consume your cannabis. Many commercial operations, for instance, prefer to trim wet. This means buds are cut away prior to drying. When you're harvesting large volumes, this method saves space. But for most home growers, we suggest drying the buds while they're still on the stem—known as "trimming dry"—it's easy and forgiving, and because the plant assists in regulating moisture, it will keep your buds from getting too parched too soon.

As always, we encourage you to do what's best for your own space and schedule, and experiment along the way. Soon, those leafy green plants in your basement will be transformed into something you can roll into a joint or pack into a pipe. But before we get to the how, we'll start with the when.

Harvesting & Trichome Development

Trichomes are the tiny, sticky hairs that cover the cannabis flower. Viewed up close, they look like crystalline mushrooms, with tall stalks and round, bulbous heads (though the latter feature only develops over time). When you hear cannabis described as "sticky," trichomes are the culprit, as they contain the vast majority of the plant's resin (and thus the vast majority of the cannabinoids and terpenes).

They're also the best indicator of when it's time to harvest. But in order to monitor their development, and their subtle changes in color, you'll need some kind of magnification. The hard-liners will insist that you need a microscope to properly monitor trichomes—we think that's probably overkill. If you've got one lying around, by all means put it to good use, but for $10 or so you can pick up a perfectly good jeweler's loupe, which is far easier to carry

around with you in your garden. (We recommend at least a 20x magnification, but 40x is ideal; if you can find one with a light, you'll make your job even easier.)

When you decide to harvest is largely dependent on two things—the strain of cannabis you're growing (different strains have different flowering times) and what kind of effect you're looking for. When it comes to the latter, everyone has their own preference, which we'd wager will become even stronger the more you experiment and understand the process.

When trichomes begin their development they're almost perfectly clear, but as they inch toward maturity, their caps begin to turn a cloudy white—an indicator that the base cannabinoid has converted into THC (somewhere in that cloudy-white stage, THC levels are at their peak). Eventually, that cloudy white will ripen into an amber hue. This is an indication that the THC is degrading and turning into CBN, which isn't as psychoactive as THC, but has its own effects and benefits, like anti-inflammatory relief or a nice afternoon nap. This progression will vary from plant to plant, based not only on the strain but also on the growing conditions. As a general rule, when you approach week 8 of flowering, it's time to start keeping a really close eye on your trichomes. The end of week 8 or the beginning of week 9 is typically the sweet spot for harvest.

It's important to clarify that you'll never have a harvest in which *every* trichome is at the exact same stage

of development; you're looking for the *majority* to reach whatever point on the spectrum you so desire, but all three stages—clear, cloudy white, and amber—will be present to some degree.

If this sounds too technical, don't fret: when you're starting out, all you really need to know is that if you're growing a sativa-dominant strain, and you want that cerebral high, harvest your cannabis when the trichomes are mostly cloudy with a few clear and *very* few amber (**1**). If you're growing an indica-heavy strain, and you're looking for a deep, relaxing body high, wait a little longer, until about 30%—but no more—of the trichomes turn amber (**2**).

When determining the right time to harvest, the only things that trump trichome development are pest infestations and destructive fungi, such as *botrytis*. If the issue can't be cleared up with the methods we suggested in the previous chapter, it's better to harvest the problem stems immediately rather than risk the rest of the plant or garden. Should you have to harvest early, don't stress. You'll still have smokable cannabis—it just won't be quite as strong. Maybe save that jar for the first time your dad comes over and wants to show you kids how they did it in his day. As some of the old hippie growers tell it, unripe cannabis will give you a headache. We've got no scientific substantiation to support that claim—only anecdotal evidence from our favorite old hippie—but we're still inclined to pass on the wisdom of our elders . . . take it or leave it!

Harvesting cannabis isn't like harvesting kale; you don't cut a few flowers here and there while it continues to bloom. When the time—and the trichome development—is right, you cut the entire plant down at the base of the stalk.

Drying

In most cases, it's simplest to dry your cannabis in the same room in which you grew it, but whatever space you choose will need to be clean, temperature- and humidity-controlled, and—when you're trimming dry—set up with some sort of structure on which to hang the plants. The easiest (and usually cheapest) options are the same ones you'd use to dry your laundry: a clothesline, a freestanding drying rack (the collapsible variety is especially convenient, as you can move it out of the way when you're not using it), or a few wire clothes hangers. So long as the plants have a good node or stem to hang from, you won't even need a clothespin.

Be sure to hang the stems so that there's sufficient air movement between them. Mimic the space between the individual buds *on* the stem—close, but not touching—as an even airflow will help with even drying. The humidity in your drying room will need to be in the range of 55–65%, and the temperature between 60 and 65°F.

We can't stress this enough: a clean room is your friend. If you have any sort of mold issues in your home, deal with them before you start growing. Mold is airborne, spreads easily, and thrives in dark, wet conditions. During the first 3 days of drying, leave the lights on in the room—this will inhibit mold inoculation while you still have excess moisture. After 3 days pass, once all of the plant cells have died and there is no longer any living matter, it's best to keep the lights off; light and heat lead to oxidation and degradation of the flowers.

Be careful where you position your drying plants. You don't want any air blowing directly over them, as this will cause them to dry unevenly; the outside will end up desiccated while the inside stays moist. You want air coming *into* the room, you want air going *out of* the room, and you want air circulating *around* the room, but you want to avoid blowing it directly onto your plants.

Depending on the size of your harvest, you can also opt for a wooden drying box, which is great for controlling moisture, temperature, and light. (It's equally useful for any number of other herbs, so if you grow mint, oregano, or basil in the summer, your drying box will help you enjoy them year-round.)

Most homes running furnaces and/or air conditioners tend to run dry—at about 40% relative humidity—so oftentimes you'll want to add some moisture to the drying box. You don't need to run out and buy an atomizing humidifier to do so; simply put a bowl of water in the box and let it slowly moisten the air. Some growers hang a clean towel inside the box with just the bottom soaking in the water. The towel helps draw the moisture out of the bowl and into the air.

Once you've got your drying room set up and your stems cut at the base, you can let time and the atmosphere do their work. The goal in drying (and in curing,

which we'll get to momentarily) is to off-gas chlorophyll while retaining flavonoids and terpenes; the slower you can dry and cure your cannabis—without inviting mold!—the better off it'll be.

The ideal moisture content for smokable cannabis is 10–15% water (when a cannabis plant is in the ground and alive, it sits at about 70%). Generally, hitting that 10–15% mark will take 5 to 7 days. If you have a plant with very large or very small flowers, of course, you'll want to adjust accordingly.

Keeping the flowers on the stalk allows them to dry more slowly than if you were to remove them and then dry them on their own. This is because the cannabis plant will continue to pull moisture through the stalk and into the flowers.

Most growers cut away the fan leaves before they hang their cannabis to dry, though others advocate leaving them on to protect the flowers from light, abrasion, dust, or that hungry moth that noticed your grow lights and found a way in. Leaves can also help the plant regulate moisture, but if you get your room's humidity right, you shouldn't need that extra help. And by leaving extra organic matter on the plant, you run a higher risk of harboring and spreading mold. At the very least, get rid of any leaves that are moldy, yellow, wilted, or otherwise unhealthy looking.

Once they're hanging, you'll want to check your drying plants twice a day by touch. Just give the bud a gentle squeeze, like you're testing produce in the supermarket—you don't want to damage the trichomes, but you'll need to get an idea of both the surface and interior conditions to make sure that the bud is drying evenly. If your cannabis dries too fast, the outside of the flowers will feel brittle, but the insides will still be wet. About 5 days after you harvest your plants, the flowers will be a little bit crunchy to the touch, and the stick will have just a little bend to it—if it snaps under minimal pressure, it's safe to assume you've dried your crop too long.

If you do find yourself with drier-than-ideal cannabis— if you pushed that stem to its breaking point—don't fret. All is not lost. You'll have a slightly harsher smoke and you'll lose some flavor. Just reach for the vaporizer this time—it tends to handle the brittle stuff better—and save your rolling papers for the next harvest (and take this opportunity to visit your local cannabis shop for something smokable; it's always good to see what the pros are up to.) At more extreme levels—say, below 5% moisture content—you will have locked in the last bit of the chlorophyll, along with that nasty hay flavor. Do your best not to let it get *that* far.

Trimming

If we were growing cannabis solely for personal consumption, we would spend far less time trimming our flowers than we do for commercial purposes. When you're trimming for the market, there are cosmetic considerations to keep in mind; when you're trimming for yourself, you need only remove those parts of the plants with no trichomes. Anything with trichomes has value—it's smokable, vaporizable, or cookable—so try not to let that hard-earned material go to waste. If you're considering making hash (which we'll discuss in Chapter Ten), you'll want a healthy pile of fan and sugar leaves. You're bound to lose trichomes while you trim, so always trim over a clean surface that can be dumped into your hash bin—a baking sheet, a TV tray, even a newspaper spread on the table will do.

We like to use bonsai scissors for trimming because their nonstick coating is resin resistant. Know that whatever scissors you use will inevitably get gunked up with residue, but oiling them after each use goes a long way. Just pour a little olive or coconut oil on a rag and wipe down any equipment that's come in contact with the plants. Many growers like to use unpowdered gloves while they trim—it keeps your hands from getting sticky and gives you that added bonus of good hygiene—but gloved or not, your hands will need a little bit of that oil as well. You won't get far without it.

STEP 1   REMOVE THE LEAVES

Begin by perfecting your grip. Hold the stem of your cola in your non-dominant hand, using about the pressure you would to hold a pencil (**1**). But be careful: dried plants are far more brittle than fresh ones, and trichomes will easily dislodge if the material is manhandled.

For your first pass, forego the sheers. Using your dominant hand, remove the large fan leaves that wrapped tightly around the buds as they dried (**2**). Find the thick stem of the fan leaf, and get your fingers as close to the base as possible without disturbing the bud. Tug the stem down and out simultaneously, snapping it off close to the main stalk. The motion of pulling the leaf requires a little finesse, but once you nail it, you'll know. Repeat until you've removed all main fan leaves (**3**). This material contains very few trichomes, and need not be saved.

STEP 2   CUT AWAY THE BUDS

Using a pair of detail trimming scissors, snip off each individual bud (**4**), making your cut right at the connection point to the main stalk. Each bud should be left with a small stem of its own (**5**); this will serve as your new handle during the more detailed manicuring stage.

Work your way from the bottom to the top (**6**). As you get into the dense main cola, discerning where each new bud starts may become difficult. Take your time and look closely to get a feel for your flower's structure—each strain is different. Don't cut too hastily, or you may slice through the center of a bud rather than clipping at the base.

STEP 3   MANICURE TIME

Hold each bud by its stem—or, if you haven't got enough room—lightly around the sides (**7**). Again, don't grip too tightly, or you'll take trichomes with you when you let go. Using your detail scissors, snip away the sugar leaves that protrude from the bud and grow out from its surface. Sugar leaves typically have a nice covering of trichomes, so be sure to set them aside. At home, we like to manicure our buds over a newspaper then tip the whole thing into a jar when we're through.

Work with your scissors at a slight angle, against the surface of the bud but also pointing in (**8**). Avoid cutting too deeply or snipping off a calyx. Start slow and shallow, make sure you have a good idea of what's sugar leaf versus what's flower. It'll seem complex at first glance, but once you start whittling away, the structure will become clear (**9**).

NOTE: Some strains, typically indicas, have very few and well pronounced sugar leaves that make for quick and straight-forward manicuring. Sativas may be trickier, as shown in our photos, with densely packed sugar leaves covering the surface. Again, each strain will be different and require you to adapt your process.

STEP 4   WHAT REMAINS

You should have four groups sorted:

- **FAN LEAVES** (**10**). Unless you're a home juicer, go ahead and compost them.

- **STICKS AND STEMS** (**11**). This is also waste material. Compost away!

- **SUGAR LEAF TRIMMINGS** (**12**). Set these aside and take advantage of the valuable trichomes by making hash (page 162), tincture (page 168), or infused butter or oil (page 193).

- **BUDS** (**13**). The fruit of your labor! Our example is a tight trim—you're free to leave a few more leaves in place if you so desire. Place them in your jar and get ready to cure.

NOTE: This particular plant is a high-CBD strain, and as a result, may have a slightly different appearance than many of the strains you're used to.

Curing

In many ways, drying cannabis is like drying any herb from your garden. Where it departs is in the curing process. Curing is about slowly drawing the moisture from the center of the flower to the outside, so that you end up with a nice, consistent bud. This allows for a high retention of volatile organic compounds (due to the low temperature) and an even consistency in moisture content. While there are a number of methods for finishing great cannabis, we've found that curing slowly at a low temperature is relatively easy to execute—and we get great results every time.

Most growers cure cannabis for at least a month, but there are some who prefer a fresher taste; one of our home-grower friends starts smoking a week after harvest because he prefers a grassier flavor. One of the joys of growing your own is that you can sample it at different stages to see what you like best. Take notes on both the flavor and experience to remind yourself what you did last time around. There are so many variables, and so much time will have elapsed between harvests; if you don't keep track, it will all start to blend together.

Once your buds are trimmed and their stems have reached that optimal bend-but-don't-break level of dryness, you'll want to store your cannabis in some sort of nonporous container with a solid seal. Make sure that it's BPA-free; you don't want anything that will leach chemicals into your buds. Terpenes will interact with non-food-grade plastics and eat away at them. We favor 5-gallon food-grade buckets with lids that snap on around the outside rim and a center component that twists on and off for easy opening. (We've found that those survival-nut websites, the kind of places that exist to fully outfit your bunker, are a great resource: the buckets are cheap, come in all different sizes, and the lids are airtight.)

Most growers think that glass is the best curing vessel. For a smaller grow, we tend to agree: glass is relatively cheap, reliably nonporous, and typically free of chemicals. The downsides are that it's breakable and heavy, and if it's clear, you'll need to leave your container in a dark place. UV rays speed up the aging process and damage the cannabinoids.

There are many ways to cure cannabis, and as usual, it's mostly a question of what's available to you and your personal preferences. Maybe you want to display your cannabis on a shelf while it cures—why not? You're proud of what you've accomplished. In that case, you may want to invest in a handsome set of violet glass jars (Miron Glass claims to use the ideal tint for blocking UV). Or maybe you'd rather reuse something you have lying around. Start saving those amber-colored plastic prescription bottles and distribute your flowers among them (though even amber shouldn't be exposed to direct sunlight for *too* long).

Stainless-steel containers are perfect for drying and curing cannabis—the Container Store, Bed Bath & Beyond, and similar big-box outlets are great resources for all of your curing needs. We've seen several people store their cannabis in lovely glass pharmacy containers, and while they might look fantastic, they have no seal, so the cannabis is bound to dry out unevenly. Find something you like, but don't sacrifice quality purely for aesthetics.

During the first week of curing, you'll want to open your container twice a day for 15 to 30 minutes—this is often called "burping." During the second week, we recommend scaling back to once a day for that same amount of time. From the third week on, 15 to 30 minutes every 2 to 3 days will suffice; any more often and you'll risk drying out your flowers.

Throughout the curing process you will walk a line between too wet and too dry. If the cannabis is trapped with too much moisture, you'll start to see mold. If, when you open your containers, your buds feel too moist, you may want to lay them out to dry for a few hours, or leave your container open overnight. If there's not enough moisture, you'll risk stopping the curing process prematurely. In this case, you might try introducing outside moisture to your vessel. One useful trick is to cut off a small corner of a brand-new sponge, wet it, and add it to the curing container. But however you add moisture, do it in small amounts incrementally over the course of a couple of days. Too much too fast and you're back in that danger zone. Once your cannabis reaches an ideal moisture level, go ahead and leave your containers closed.

MOISTURE CONTROL PACKETS

Whether you're trying to add or remove moisture during curing, or just want a fail-safe once you've decided your cannabis is ready to sit undisturbed in that sealed container, two-way moisture control packets are an excellent solution. (They're also great for long-term storage.) Boveda is currently the most popular brand, but there are other manufacturers out there. These small, inexpensive devices keep your cannabis at just the right moisture level—they're popular with cigar smokers, who use them in their humidors. After the first week of curing, we often add Boveda packets to our buckets to make sure the flowers aren't drying too fast. The packets are rated by their relative humidity—the ones that we use are rated 62%. That's on the moist end of where most people want their cannabis, but at this point, it's the lowest level they've got. (If and when they start making a 57% humidity packet, that one will get our ringing endorsement.)

Even after that first month, when the buds are sufficiently cured, we recommend that anyone storing cannabis for longer than 3 months use a Boveda packet. They cost about $5 and guarantee that you don't find yourself smoking the skeletal remains of your hard-earned crop. How long the packets last depends on how often you open the container, but in our experience, it's usually about 6 months. You can tell when the packet is on its last legs because the gel inside starts to congeal. (They're similar to those hand-warmer packets you might have used on ski trips—when they've exhausted themselves they harden up and feel like little sacks of rocks.)

So long as you're not in danger of mold, it's better to be on the moist side than the dry side; as with a bad haircut, you can always take a little more off the top.

Storage

You're probably excited to sample your crop, and in the next few chapters, we'll teach you everything you need to know about enjoying your newly harvested buds. But pace yourself—not too much at once! Most of your stash should be carefully stowed away, and the best way to store your cured flower is in a lightproof or tinted container at 60–75°F. The most sensitive time is over, but with too much exposure to the air or too much heat, you still run the risk of letting your THC oxidize and convert to CBN. In average room-temperature environments, even with a container that's not particularly airtight, you shouldn't see too much degradation, but why risk it? Don't leave your cured cannabis in clear glass where UV rays can get to it, and certainly don't store it in your glove box or anywhere else susceptible to extreme heat. We trust you'll use your common sense.

If you're a home grower who doesn't smoke very often, and you harvest 3 pounds of flowers, that might take you about 10 years to work through. If you stored it all in one big bucket, opening it each time you wanted a hit, after a couple of years you'd be smoking some pretty heavy CBN. A better strategy is to portion those 3 pounds into a number of smaller vessels, or store the bulk of your cannabis in a large container that you open up once every few months—just often enough to refresh your regularly accessed supply.

If you find that your buds are drier than you'd prefer, take a small piece of orange peel and leave it in your container overnight (just don't forget about it in there—it's not too late for mold to ruin your party). That little bit of moisture can do wonders for thirsty cannabis.

And now, finally, the fun part . . .

9

Chapter Ten

CANNABIS IN ALL
ITS FORMS

IF THE LAST TIME YOU PURCHASED WEED WAS FROM YOUR FRIEND'S COUSIN'S coworker, walking into a modern cannabis shop may be a bit jarring. That's not to say that many retailers aren't outfitted to look like your hippie neighbor's basement—a variety of aesthetics do and *should* exist—but many of the best operations are closer in feel to a third-wave coffee shop or a high-end pharmacy. You'll be able to browse dozens of strains and numerous products, and—if you're lucky—an educated, friendly neighborhood budtender will help you find just what you need for a quiet weeknight with your record collection, a hike with your friends, or that nagging pain in your lower back.

But whether you're preparing to sample your first batch of homegrown bud or getting ready to scour a menu of cannabis concentrates, we thought it would be helpful to have a primer on your options—all of cannabis's glorious forms. In this chapter, we'll walk you through the end results of cannabis production, from products you'll be able to whip up at home from your personal harvest to those best left to the professionals and purchased from your local cannabis shop. In the next chapter, we'll catalog the various methods of consuming each of these forms. You'll notice edibles are noticeably missing from both lists—not to worry: we've given them Chapter Twelve all to themselves.

Flower

This is usable cannabis in its most straightforward form. It's what you've browsed for in shops and dispensaries, what you've purchased from the delivery guy, and—if you've taken advantage of the previous chapters—what you've got waiting for you in those curing containers.

The cannabis flower is home to the highest concentration of the plant's trichomes. (For those of you who flipped to the back of the book to see how it ends: trichomes are the resinous glands that produce cannabis's gold mine of cannabinoids and terpenes.) The sugar leaves can contain respectable concentrations as well—and we'll get to what the prudent grower can do with them—but the vast majority of cannabis consumed in this country comes in the form of dried, cured, and manicured buds. In Chapter Two we gave you a primer on subspecies and strains, and walked you through the assorted cannabinoids and terpenes that give each strain its particular effects and flavors. Still, there are a few things that are helpful to keep in mind when you're buying or consuming flower.

CHOOSING GOOD BUD

SMELL/FLAVOR: Pay attention to what your senses tell you. When you smell or taste something you like, that's your body responding positively. Note what terpenes are present, so you can seek them out in other strains. Each strain has its own unique bouquet, but if it smells harsh, hardly smells at all—or if it has taken on the smell of its storage vessel—that's a good indication that the flower is lacking or that it's been improperly stored.

TEXTURE: You're not looking for wet flower—that's asking for mold—but if your bud feels dry and brittle, it's probably not at its peak. This isn't to say it's unusable (we even have a recommendation for reintroducing moisture on page 155), but it's not worth top dollar.

THE EYEBALL TEST: As you get to know a strain, you'll have a better idea of its particular colors and trichome density, but there *are* some universal cues: Are you seeing a lot of stem or excess leaf? There's nothing wrong with these in and of themselves, but it means you're not getting much bang for your buck. Heavy on the seeds? Not the end of the world, but an indication of lower-quality flower.

REPUTATION: The legal cannabis industry is new, and many growers are still working out their best practices. Do your research and talk to your budtenders, lest you learn the hard way about the dangers of pesticides and other harmful toxins.

Kief

When trichomes are separated from the cannabis plant, the result is a fine, powdery substance known as kief (also referred to as "dry sieve hash"). While it might be most notable for its use in hash production, don't sleep on kief in its raw, stand-alone form. You can sprinkle it over the flower in your joint or bowl, you can add it to your vaporizer, you can use it for cooking, or you can stir it into your morning coffee or tea (the heat decarboxylates the cannabinoids and thereby activates them).

Loose kief usually has a light sandy color—it darkens considerably when pressed into hash. If your kief has a greenish tint, that usually means it contains plant matter in addition to those precious trichomes; this is in no way harmful, but signifies a less potent product.

SCREEN YOUR OWN

A three-chamber grinder with a screen will collect kief over time. But if you're growing your own and want to take advantage of your trimmings, consider investing in a series of stainless-steel screens, each slightly denser than the last. You can buy products online specific to this purpose—they usually have a drawer or receptacle beneath the screen to catch your haul—or you can track down a supplier of screen-printing supplies and make your own. Steel mesh is measured either in lines per square inch (LPI) or in microns (one-millionth of a meter). With LPI, the higher the number, the finer the mesh; with microns, it's the opposite. For kief collection, most people opt for a range of 100–270 LPI or 50–150 microns.

Start by placing your trim on the coarsest mesh. Agitate the plant material by jiggling the screen, then gently rub it against the mesh—not too hard, as you don't want to grind too much of the plant into your kief. Repeat the process with your finer screens until you're satisfied with the color and texture.

Keep in mind that if your cannabis is too moist, it will have a hard time releasing the trichomes; if it's too brittle, you'll end up with excess plant matter making its way through your screen.

10

Hash

Derived from the Arabic word for "grass," hash (or hashish) has been produced and used for thousands of years throughout the Middle East and China. (It didn't gain popularity here in the States until the 1960s.)

Hash is a processed version of kief, and while there are numerous methods for making it—both manual and with a machine—most involve a combination of pressure and heat. The idea is to meld the individual trichomes into a solid form.

Because it contains little to no plant matter, hash is significantly higher in cannabinoid content than flower. It ranges in color from gold to dark brown, and in texture from dry and powdery to sticky and putty-like. Hash is typically smoked or vaporized—usually mixed with tobacco or cannabis flower, since it has difficulty burning on its own—but it can also be used in cooking. Once hash is pressed—as long as the kief wasn't too wet—it keeps remarkably well. As with cannabis flower, your best bet is to keep it in a cool, dark place.

BUBBLE HASH

One popular method of hash production is through a process called ice-water extraction. (It's also a great way to separate and utilize the precious trichomes from all your leftover trim and shake.) The end result is called bubble (or water) hash. Plant material is placed in a filtration bag along with water and ice. The bag is heavily agitated, which helps to separate the trichomes from the plant, then left alone for 3 to 6 hours to settle. (**NOTE**: Ice water is essential, as it keeps the resin glands from becoming too soft and sticky, and it helps to separate the trichomes from the plant during agitation.) The lighter plant material will float to the top, while the heavier resin glands will fall through the filter and settle in the lower portion. Once dried, water hash is similar to the kief you'd collect from screening, and likewise can be used on its own or in traditional hash production.

If you're interested in water hash, the easiest way to get started is by buying a set of prefab bags. (They'll run you anywhere from $40–$300.) Each manufacturer has its own set of instructions, but don't be surprised—or frustrated—if it takes a bit of trial and error to get it just right.

PRESS YOUR OWN

BY HAND:

Sprinkle a gram or two of kief in the palm of one hand, then apply pressure with the other. Once the powder starts to solidify, knead it with your thumb for 15 to 20 minutes, until you have a solid ball or wafer.

IN YOUR SHOE:

Wrap a couple of grams of kief tightly in cellophane, put it in the bottom of your shoe, then go about your business for an hour or two. By the time you unlace your sneakers, the heat and pressure will have done their work.

WITH A BOTTLE:

Place a few grams of kief inside a folded sheet of cellophane. Fill a wine bottle with hot water and roll it back and forth over the kief as if it were cookie dough until, again, you have a solid wafer.

10

Rosin

In terms of cannabis concentrates, rosin is the new kid on the block. The end result looks much like the kind of extraction you get with solvent-based methods—it has either a sappy or waxy texture—but rosin is produced with a simple mechanical process of applied heat and pressure.

With proper execution, rosin retains levels of potency and flavor similar to those achieved with other extraction methods, but there's still research to be done in terms of its retention of some of cannabis's essential oils (at least compared to CO_2 extraction). That said, if given the choice between rosin and harsher solvent-based concentrates—butane, we're looking at you—we'll take rosin every time. It can be used in a vaporizer, with a dab rig, or even be added to a joint.

While commercial producers are using industrial-sized presses, it's possible to produce rosin with simple household items. If you've got a hair straightener, a roll of parchment paper, and an oven mitt, you're most of the way there.

MAKE YOUR OWN

1. Heat your hair straightener to somewhere between 250 and 300°F (any higher and you'll begin to damage the terpenes).

2. Place your flower inside a folded sheet of parchment paper and—wearing your oven mitt or safety gloves—place it between the straightener's irons.

3. Squeeze the straightener as tight as you can for 5 to 7 seconds, then remove and open the parchment paper.

4. Your flower should have secreted a small amount of golden ooze. Wait for it to cool and solidify; then—using a dab tool or any fine metal instrument—collect your rosin.

REMEMBER: This is potent concentrate; a little goes a long way.

Solvent-Based Concentrates

There are getting to be as many names for concentrates as there are for grass—*shatter, budder, honeycomb, wax*. Most attempt to describe color and texture, and there's certainly a variety of each. But neither characteristic can tell you precisely the process that was used in a concentrate's production. Solvent-based extraction creates consistencies ranging from oil to something like glass and everything inbetween—and none of them are *necessarily* indicators of quality. Concentrates are used in pen cartridges, with dab rigs, or simply sprinkled or smeared onto ground flower before smoking or vaporizing. (We'll get into the finer points of using concentrates in the next chapter.)

But not all solvent-based concentrates are created equal. And while they're all capable of getting you tremendously stoned, some have significantly more downsides and risks than others. Given that our industry is relatively new, we're still working with limited research, testing, and regulation. We don't know the long-term effects of ingesting some of the chemicals commonly used in commercial concentrates. If you are unsure whether a product you are considering is safe, and the manufacturer neglects to disclose the results of its lab tests, you might opt for another of cannabis's many forms.

ALCOHOL SOLVENT EXTRACTION
RSO, ISO, Phoenix Tears—these oils use alcohol solvents to extract the resin from the trichromes, then the solution is strained thoroughly and cooked at a low temperature until the solvent is evaporated. Once that solvent is purged, the finished product is a dark, viscous—and quite potent—oil.

But! A few words of warning: The most common alcohol used in this method—isopropyl—is highly flammable and can be dangerous if not heated correctly. It's also a poison. Most alcohol solvents are either inherently poisonous or—as with denatured spirits—have chemicals added to render them undrinkable. While it's certainly possible to remove all trace elements from your final product, it's a difficult and laborious process. (And the only way you'll know for sure whether it's been done is with a lab test.) If this is your cannabis product of choice, you might consider using ethanol as your solvent. It may be cost prohibitive—and it's still difficult to purge—but

---

THE LAST DROP

HELPFUL HINT: To get the last of that sticky concentrate out of its jar, simply run the sealed jar under hot water or hit it with a shot of hot air from a blow-dryer. You can also pop the jar in the freezer for an hour, then pry your frozen concentrate loose.

10

ethanol is safe to ingest and has the distinct advantage of not risking the destruction of your nervous system.

Whichever solvent you choose, the purging process will most likely destroy the most volatile terpenes and cannabinoids; it also tends to pull chlorophyll from the plant material, which results in an unpleasant taste. Therefore, we can't vouch for the quality or safety of this particular kind of concentrate. And while we likewise can't vouch for cannabis activist and RSO namesake Rick Simpson's claims that ISO—ingested and applied topically—cured his metastatic skin cancer, we can point you toward his official website (phoenixtears.ca), which contains both his argument for ISO's medical benefits and his detailed instructions for making it.

BHO

In recent years, butane hash oil (BHO) has become one of the most popular concentrates on the market—perhaps due to its extremely high levels of THC. The better producers are able to retain a strain's particular terpene profile, but often such subtleties are lost in the process.

BHO, like other concentrates, comes in a range of consistencies. Liquid variations are used in vape cartridges, but these are usually cut with propylene glycol or vegetable glycerin to retain their liquescence. Wax is an easier-to-handle form created by agitating or whipping the BHO during the purging process. Shatter is the most refined version, and usually requires a vacuum oven in order to extract the waxes, lipids, and trace solvents. Shatter is typically the texture of hard candy, with colors ranging from yellow to amber. It can be used in many vaporizers, but it's especially popular with the dab-rig crowd.

As you may have guessed, we tend to avoid butane concentrates, as there's very little data on the long-term effects of even trace amounts of the solvent. And if you're considering bypassing the professionals, know that BHO is dangerous to produce. It requires highly complicated techniques and highly volatile solvents—just ask anyone working at a burn treatment center, where cases of serious injuries related to hash oil production have been skyrocketing over the last few years. For those reasons, we won't get into the process specifics here, but if you are planning to use BHO, please make sure you're procuring it from a reputable source.

CO_2

Our favorites of the bunch—and the ones we've put our time, energy, and resources into producing—CO_2 concentrates have all the benefits (and pleasures) of BHO without the residual solvents, which leaves you with as pure an extraction as possible. It can get closer to a full-spectrum concentrate, preserving all of the characteristics of your chosen strain. Again, this probably isn't something to do at home—it takes expensive and specialized equipment—but it's well worth your dime the next time you stop in to your neighborhood shop.

CO_2 concentrates come in all the same forms as their butane brethren, but to produce them carbon dioxide is compressed to create a supercritical or subcritical fluid, which acts as a solvent to extract essential oils, waxes, and lipids from the cannabis. (A similar methodology is used in the essential oils industry to produce aromatic lavender, rosemary, sandalwood, etc.) Temperature and pressure must be calibrated to specific standards in order to preserve the delicate cannabinoids and terpenes.

Right now there seems to be a huge range in the quality of CO_2 cannabis oils on the market. Many producers are trying to replicate the results of BHO solvents, and use temperatures and pressures that maximize THC. That's all well and good, but it usually means destroying other valuable, more sensitive constituents that add to the overall effect of the strain. Similarly, cannabinoids and terpenes can be lost through secondary purging processes. Another solvent—usually grain alcohol—is added to the concentrate and then purged, taking with it the fats and waxes that made up the original concentrate and lessened its purity. As with most things, you have to choose your battles. Generally speaking, we'd rather leave those fats and waxes in our concentrate than sacrifice the overall integrity of the strain.

Tinctures

One of the easiest ways to consume cannabis—a few beads from a medicine dropper and you're good for a couple of hours—is also one of the easiest ways to prepare it. Tinctures use alcohol to extract cannabinoids from plant material. You decarb your cannabis, soak it in a high-proof spirit, and then strain the leftover plant material. This can be accomplished gradually over 4 to 6 weeks or—with a couple of extra steps—in as little as an hour. (We'll walk you through both timelines.)

Expect the high to come on quicker than with most edibles, but slower than when you smoke or vaporize (similarly, the duration of the high is somewhere in between). Tinctures are available in many dispensaries and recreational shops, but are easy to make from flower itself or from your leftover trim, shake, and leaves. Store-bought tinctures will often come with a recommended dosage, but if you've made your own, start with a couple of drops the first time—either sublingually (under your tongue) or in a beverage—so you can gauge its strength . . . it's not fun to overdo it.

Cannabis Tincture

1. Preheat your oven to 240°F.

2. Grind ¼ oz. of flower in a coffee grinder or small food processor. (If you're using trim, you'll want 2 oz.; with leaf, you'll want 4 oz.)

3. On a shallow baking sheet, heat your ground plant material for 40 minutes, stirring every 10.

4. Place the cannabis in a wide-mouth jar, and pour in 4 fl. oz. of high proof spirits (Everclear, Bacardi 151, etc.).

FOR QUICK TINCTURE: Under an oven fan (or, better, outdoors on a hot plate), set your uncovered mason jar in a warm water bath and insert a thermometer. Let simmer at no higher than 165°F for 30 minutes. (**WARNING**: Pure alcohol boils at 173°F. DO NOT let it reach that point—high-proof spirits are flammable and potentially dangerous.)

FOR SLOW-AND-STEADY TINCTURE: Seal your jar, shake vigorously, and store in a cool, dark place for 4 to 6 weeks, shaking every day or two.

5. Place a piece of cheesecloth over your jar and strain spirits into a large liquid measuring cup. Collect the remaining plant material inside the cheesecloth and squeeze to extract any remaining liquid.

6. Carefully fill a glass dropper bottle, clearly label it—so as not to confuse it with your echinacea—and enjoy.

Topicals & Transdermals

It's only natural that a plant rich in both healing properties and essential oils would find its way into the world of lotions, sprays, and balms. The medical market has provided such products for some time, but as the recreational cannabis industry has taken off, we've seen more and more exciting options. Topicals and transdermals are great for relieving headaches, increasing blood flow, easing muscle soreness and inflammation—even soothing post-tattoo skin pain.

Most of the cannabinoids that are active in flower or concentrates are present in topicals—many manufacturers will try to replicate the balance of terpenes and cannabinoids from particular strains—but since they are absorbed into skin tissue and don't breach the bloodstream, the effects tend to be nonpsychoactive and noncerebral. This also means the benefits are hyperlocalized; the cannabinoids bind to CB2 receptors wherever the topical is applied. Lotion or balm might be perfect for someone who wants the therapeutic benefits of cannabis without the psychoactive ones. But these products aren't just for pain management; recently, we've even seen the emergence of cannabis-infused sensual massage oils and personal lubricants.

Cannabis transdermals—such as patches—are often used by people who want to take advantage of cannabis's broader benefits, but cannot or do not wish to smoke, vaporize, or ingest it. Unlike topicals, transdermals deliver the cannabinoids directly into the bloodstream, which affords the highest rate of absorption. It also allows the effects to be felt throughout the body. Many—though certainly not all—transdermals are nonpsychoactive, and vary in terms of time release from 6 to 36 hours. You'll typically start feeling the effects after about 45 minutes; if the experience is not to your liking, once you remove the patch, the effects will mostly diminish in about an hour. Newer to the market—and similar insofar as they allow the cannabinoids to enter the bloodstream quickly—are vaginal suppositories (aka "the weed tampon"), which have become popular for easing menstrual cramps. The cannabinoids have a twofold effect: assuaging nerve endings in the uterus, cervix, and ovaries while also sending more pleasant signals to the brain. For all transdermals, if you have preexisting medical conditions it's probably worth talking with your healthcare provider before you dive in.

10

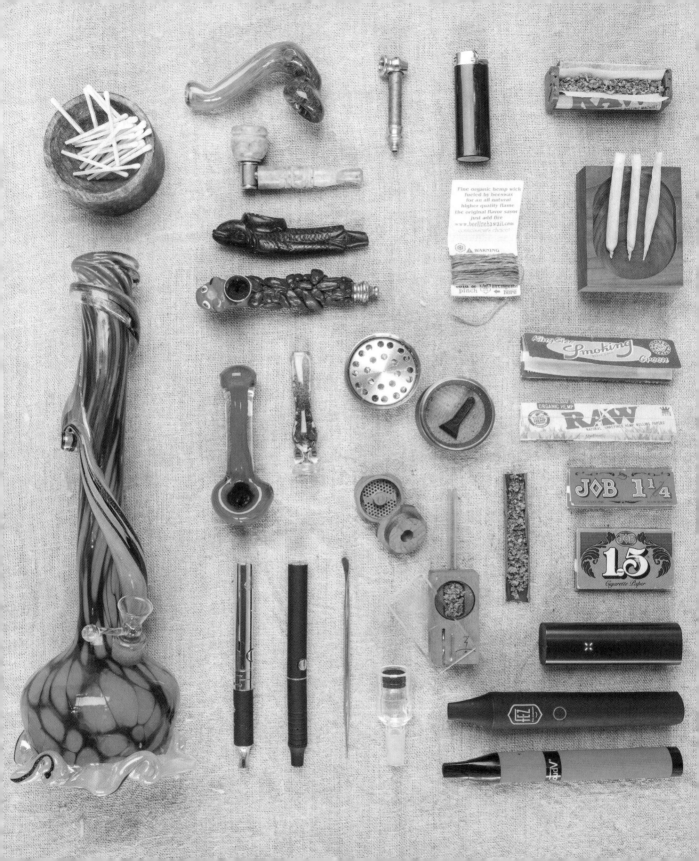

Chapter Eleven

CONSUMING YOUR CANNABIS

THERE ARE MYRIAD METHODS FOR ENJOYING CANNABIS: FROM THE HUMBLEST roach to glass pipes worthy of a Chihuly retrospective; from Silicon Valley fetish objects to baked goods that would make Jacquy Pfeiffer proud. In the previous chapter, we ran through a variety of cannabis forms—your flower, your concentrates, even your suppositories—and discussed their benefits and differences. Likewise, every manner of consuming cannabis will alter the experience: some are easier on the lungs; some are more cost-efficient; some help you avoid particular side effects; some are more potent (read: they'll get you *real* stoned). It's also important to remember that cannabinoids and terpenes react differently depending on the temperature at which they're decarboxylated.

But chemistry aside, we all have our own personal preferences. They can be informed by nostalgia and ritual as much as anything else. Some circumstances call for a hit on the sly while others are best enjoyed with a rip from a four-foot bong. Wherever you find yourself on the spectrum, we've got you covered.

We'll teach you how to roll a joint, carve a pipe from an apple, and make your own gravity bong. We'll catalog various smoking implements and offer tips wherever we can—everything from proper etiquette to proper cleaning. It won't take long to figure out what you like and what you'd like to avoid. In the meantime, take a puff and pass to the left.

Roll It

A doobie. A jazz cigarette. A jay, a jimjam, a fatty. Whatever name you choose, it entails grinding your cannabis and rolling it into a tight little cylinder. But even your standard rolling papers vary: they range in size (the bigger the paper, the bigger the joint), thickness (heavier paper means a slower burn), and even material (tobacco, wood pulp, rice paper, hemp, or natural plant cellulose). Much of the distinction comes down to feel, so experiment with the various options and see which ones you like best. We've got a handy guide to rolling on pages 174–175, but first, let's discuss the key players.

THE JOINT

Burn. One. Down. The old standby. Finely ground flower rolled evenly and snug. A perfectly rolled joint brings a sense of satisfaction, and while it may not be the showiest of party tricks, it's always a welcome skill. You'll want somewhere in the neighborhood of a half gram of flower, preferably sticky enough to hold its shape once you've worked it between your thumb and forefinger. Avoid any stem, as it runs the risk of poking a hole in your paper. We recommend using a paper crutch that allows you to smoke all the way to the end without burning your fingers. Simply light one end, drag from the other, and pass to your left.

THE ENHANCED JOINT

Those with a high tolerance (or in want of more flavor) might lace their flower with hash or cannabis concentrates. The easiest method is to sprinkle a small amount of kief over your bud. Prep your paper *before* you add the cannabis: just place a thin strip of concentrate down the center of your paper, then cover it in flower (this will spare you a mess when it comes to rolling).

A more ornate technique—if your concentrate has a firmer "pull-and-snap" texture—involves coiling a strip around the outside of the joint. Just roll out the concentrate until it's as thin as angel-hair pasta, then wind

WHEN IN ROME
(OR PARIS, OR AMSTERDAM . . .)

To confuse the matter a bit further, across the Atlantic, the meanings of "joint" and "spliff" are swapped. If you're offered a joint in Europe, it will most likely contain tobacco. Many Europeans will refer to any joint rolled in a larger cone shape—the kind of pre-rolls you might buy at a dispensary—as a spliff. Regional vernacular applies in the States as well; everyone has developed their own language for talking about cannabis, and it's ever evolving. Never be afraid to ask!

it around the joint 3 or 4 times. But careful: don't roll too far past the center of the joint, or it may get messy, and you need to rotate the joint as it burns, so as not to drip hot wax on your hands. We want to emphasize that enhanced joints aren't *just* for those smokers looking for extra potency; we recommend them as a way to mix strains—taking advantage of their different properties—and to infuse your standard fare with something higher in CBD.

THE SPLIFF

The joint's continental cousin uses your standard rolling papers, but contains a combination of cannabis and tobacco. Spliff loyalists celebrate the way it allows them to control for potency—plus it makes your stash last a little longer. Start with a thin layer of tobacco, then sprinkle your ground flower evenly on top (ratios vary widely according to taste, but if you're not a tobacco smoker already, you might want to steer clear of it entirely). Roll it just like you would a joint, crutch and all.

THE BLUNT

Cigar aficionados might bypass rolling papers and opt instead for the tobacco-leaf wrapper of their favorite bodega-brand stogies. You simply make a lengthwise incision, gently empty out the tobacco therein, replace it with your ground flower, then roll it much like you would a joint. Again, if you're not already a tobacco smoker, this one may hit you hard. The heady, up-front effects of the nicotine bring a more immediate dimension to the high.

HEMP WICKS: Some smokers have an aversion to bringing a lighter straight to their herb—directly inhaling butane fumes is bad for your health and lighter flint can contaminate your stash. Waxed-hemp twine makes for a cleaner smoke, and since it burns at a lower temperature, you'll preserve more cannabinoids and terpenes. Hemp wicks are easy to use and a 20-foot roll will cost you all of $5.

PRE-ROLLS

All the convenience and portability of a joint with none of the work! Buyer beware, the old adage "You get what you pay for" is especially true here. Don't get waylaid by distinctions like "all flower." It's more useful just to ask the shop which joint is burning the smoothest and tastiest. The biggest factor we've found in the pre-roll market comes down to curing. Joints filled with properly cured cannabis have a smooth, flavorful smoke; those that aren't make for a harsh, burnt taste.

11

ROLL YOUR OWN

STEP 1 GRIND YOUR FLOWER

Whether you use your hands (**2**), a card (**3**), or a grinder (**4**), the more uniform the bud (**1**) is ground, the more evenly your joint will burn. Be sure to pick out any seeds (they'll pop) or stems (no matter how small, they'll tear your paper).

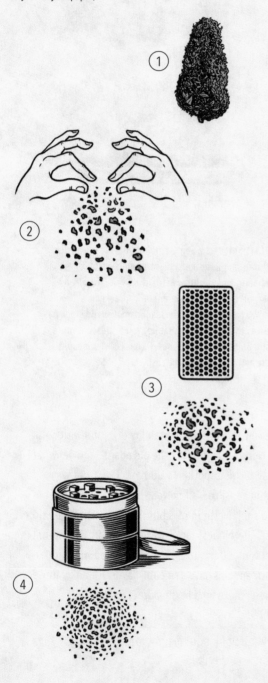

STEP 2 ROLL YOURSELF A CRUTCH

This will serve as a pseudo-filter and allow you to smoke to the end of the joint without burning your fingers. Start with a strip of thick, sturdy paper, crimp the end twice (**1**), and roll into a neat cylinder (**2**).

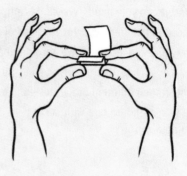

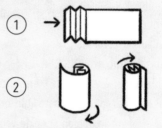

STEP 3 ASSEMBLE THE PARTS

With the glue strip of your rolling paper facing up, place the crutch at the center of one end, slightly hanging off the edge. Spread your cannabis out in a cone shape that tapers toward the crutch side. This will aid the shape of your joint as you roll. Beginners beware! Most papers only hold ½ gram–1 gram of material.

STEP 4   SHAPE AND PACK

Fold the paper in half (hot-dog style), and hold each end between the tips of your thumbs and forefingers, just above the cannabis. Roll back and forth, compressing the material but maintaining that slight cone shape. Not too tight—airflow through the material allows for a steady burn.

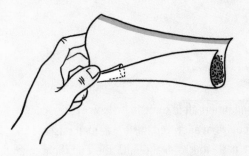

STEP 5   ROLL YOUR JOINT

Tuck the unglued edge of the paper around the crutch. Using just a little bit of moisture, tack down your glue strip around the crutch end—this will serve as your guide—then tuck and roll your way down the length of the joint. Finally, lick the glue strip as a final seal.

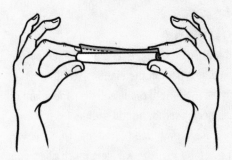

STEP 6   TEND TO THE ENDS

Using a pencil—or whatever you have handy—gently pack down the cannabis in the open end of the joint. You'll also want to press the crutch the rest of the way into the joint, so it's flush with the end of your papers.

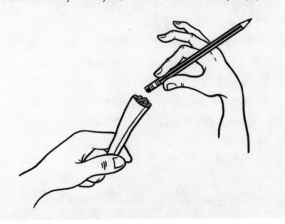

STEP 7   TAP IT

Lightly tap the crutch end on your rolling surface; this helps to even out the density of the joint.

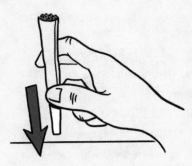

STEP 8   CLOSE IT

Twist or fold the excess paper. (If you're going to smoke right away and there's no risk of spilling your precious flower, you're free to skip this step.)

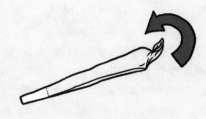

STEP 9   SPARK IT

Hold a flame to the end of the joint, slowly rotating the latter, until you have a nice, even cherry. Once it's lit, take a hit and pass to your left!

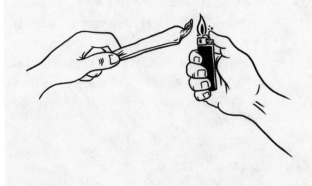

Pack It

THE CLASSIC PIPE

Your standard pipe comes in a variety of shapes, sizes, and materials, but the fundamentals are the same: a bowl, a stem, a mouthpiece, and a carburetor (or "carb"). The latter is a small hole on the side of the bowl that helps control the flow of air and smoke. You cover the carb with your thumb as you light the cannabis and draw smoke into the stem, then release it once the flower is well-lit and rolling—this allows you to easily inhale the rest of the smoke from the chamber.

The most popular variations on this theme are the straight pipe (or spoon) and the Sherlock (or Gandalf, depending on your taste in genre fiction). Historically, they were made out of wood or unfinished clay because of the unique tastes that these materials imparted to the smoking flavor. Today, as cultivators and smokers have become more interested in the varied flavor profiles of their cannabis, neutral materials—namely glass—have become more popular.

THE ONE-HITTER

When you need something small, something discreet—something that fits in your watch pocket— try a one-hitter (also known as a "bat" or a "oneie"). Shaped like—and often designed to resemble—a cig- arette, this concert-and-ballpark standby is made for one glorious hit (though you can usually manage a

few). One-hitters often come in their own cases, known as dugouts, that allow you to store a small stash.

Just pack your cannabis into the end, light, and inhale. There is no carb—so the smoke is not easily cleared—but you'll want to be careful not to breathe *too* deeply, as your spent flower can easily turn into a mouth- ful of ash. Finally, one-hitters are short and can quickly get piping hot—be careful not to burn your lips.

THE CHILLUM

Though it may sound like the term was coined by Ven- ice Beach stoners back in the eighties, "chillum" is de- rived from the Hindi word *cilam*, and the simple, conical design has been used by Hindu sadhus for centuries. Made from glass, clay, wood, or stone, chillums vary widely in size (and that size will very much affect your smoking experience).

The clumsier among us might use it just like a one-hitter, but we'd be remiss if we didn't walk you through the proper technique. Hold the chillum upright with the bowl at the top. Make a fist around the pipe with one hand while cupping the other underneath the mouthpiece (it'll look like you just threw *rock* in Rock, Paper, Scissors). While a friend lights the cannabis, draw air from the crack between your pinky finger and your palm; your mouth needn't touch the mouthpiece.

GRINDERS

You can get by without a grinder—scissors, knives, or simply your fingers will do in a pinch—but if you've spent any time carefully picking apart stems from your bud, you know it's a worthwhile luxury. Our preference is a simple aluminum three-chamber rotary grinder. The first chamber is dotted with metal teeth to grind the flower; the second is outfitted with a sieve for filtering the stray trichomes; and the third is for collecting them. Just place your flower in the first chamber and give it a few twists until the bud is sufficiently broken apart. (These work perfectly well for culinary herbs and spices as well: just be sure to rinse thoroughly before and after using—especially if you're cooking for your in-laws.)

(Many chillum users wrap the mouthpiece in a thin, wet cloth, which not only creates a filter but also keeps the pipe from getting too hot.)

Chillum etiquette dictates that the person who prepares the pipe does not partake first, and if the chillum is significant or special, the owner will be the one to clean it.

THE STEAMROLLER

Somewhere between the classic pipe and the more sophisticated bubbler, steamrollers are usually glass tubes open at both ends and fitted with a bowl on the top. The end opposite the mouthpiece acts as the carb, and the pipe is shaped to allow smoke to be "rolled" and cooled within the chamber. This guy isn't for beginners—it's known for hard, hot rips—but once you've got it down, it's a great smoking device.

THE BUBBLER

So far we've been dealing with air and fire, but this pipe adds H_2O to the mix. The bubbler uses a water-filled chamber—placed below the bowl—to diffuse the smoke before it reaches the stem and eventually your lungs. Bubblers are known for their smooth, clean hits, as the water filters out much of that harsh tar and resin taste.

Most people add cold water to their bubblers to calm the bronchial passages. Others prefer hot water in order to add vapor to the equation, which can open up your airways and allow for more smoke to enter. Whatever temperature you choose, be careful not to spill or swallow—all that tar and resin have to get stuck somewhere.

THE BONG

The tabletop version of the bubbler, the bong operates on the same basic principles. A bong pulls smoke through water to produce a filtered toke that's easier on the throat and lungs. Bongs are made up of four components: the water chamber, the tube, the downstem, and the bowl. The water chamber is usually positioned at the base of the bong and acts as its central nervous system—controlling and connecting everything. A tube leads from the water chamber to an opening at the top, which serves as a mouthpiece. The downstem is a small removable pipe that protrudes diagonally from the water chamber; at its peak is the bowl into which you place your flower.

To use a bong, fill the chamber until the surface of the water is above the bottom of the downstem. Fill

11

your bowl with flower and position your lips inside the mouthpiece, creating something of a seal with your cheeks. Light the flower, and draw the smoke through the water until the tube is full. Pull the downstem out of the chamber—this has the same effect as releasing your thumb from a carb—and inhale.

The larger the bong's tube, the more room for smoke—you'll want to take into consideration how that might affect your experience. Though the bong's signature look is tall, straight, blown glass, there are all sorts of variations. The percolator bong, for instance, features a second water chamber, which is suspended above the waterline and provides additional filtration. The recycler bong is engineered to allow you to refilter your smoke using multiple chambers.

CLEANING

You wouldn't pour a good Barolo into an unwashed milk glass. Why would you smoke your hard-won cannabis out of a dirty pipe? Along with being unhygienic and unattractive, tar and resin buildup can lead to an altered flavor profile. Luckily, cleaning your tools is pretty straightforward.

Boiling is best for glass, metal, or solid ceramic pieces; it gets at all of the buildup that can't be accessed via spot cleaning. Cover your piece with room temperature water (dropping a cold object into hot water is a recipe for thermal shock and shattering), then tilt it back and forth to be sure there are no trapped pockets of air. Gradually bring the water to a boil, making sure that the piece doesn't move around too much and risk cracking.

When you're satisfied with the resin removal—it typically takes around 20 minutes—turn off the heat and

BONG DOs & DON'Ts

DON'T SPILL!
Dirty, stagnant bong water will ruin your carpet and your buzz.

HANDLE WITH CARE!
Most bongs are big, delicate glass sculptures. They're flat on the bottom for a reason—leave them safe and sound on a level surface . . . and beware of your cat.

INHALE ONLY!
If you exhale into your mouthpiece, you risk pushing water through the stem and ruining your flower.

THE BIGGER, THE BETTER!
The bigger the water chamber—not necessarily the tube—the longer the filtration water will stay cool and clean, which results in a fresher taste.

WASTE NOT, WANT NOT!
As long as there's smoke in the bong, cup your hand over the mouthpiece until you're ready for another go (or pass it along to someone who is).

STALE SMOKE = HARSH VIBES
Smoke becomes stale quickly—we're talking a few seconds. In a pipe with a large glass chamber, you can actually watch the color of the smoke darken as it degrades. Smaller devices tend to provide you with cleaner smoke, as you're able to clear the chamber more quickly. If you're tempted by a large chamber, just be sure that the carb is big enough that you can clear the smoke before it starts to turn.

11

allow both pipe and water to cool down. After 10 to 15 minutes, grab some kitchen tongs and gently agitate the piece under the water to dislodge any remaining clumps of buildup. Dump the water from the pot, and refill it with clean warm water and a little dish soap. Using a pipe cleaner or brush, give your piece a good scrub, then let it dry on a clean towel. (**HOT TIP:** Don't use a good kitchen pot! Head to Goodwill or dig into the back of your cupboard, and grab something you don't mind decorating with a little resin-ring.)

Solvent cleaning is also an option for most glass, metal, and finished ceramic pieces, but be sure to do a spot test ahead of time to be certain that the material will not be damaged. Mix 2 parts 91% (or higher) isopropyl alcohol and one part salt; the alcohol dissolves the resin and the salt provides abrasion in order to loosen it. We'll also bang the drum again for d-limonene—that wonderful and naturally occurring solvent—which can be used in place of alcohol (especially for spot cleaning).

Place your piece in a sealable plastic bag, cover it with solvent mix, and then shake and agitate for several minutes. Remove the pipe and take care of any detail work with a cotton swab. Once you've given your piece a thorough once-over, give it one more round in the bag with fresh solvent, rinse the piece in water, and let it dry on a clean towel.

ONE IMPORTANT CAVEAT: If you're using a bubbler, it's best to keep a small film of resin intact. If the inside of your bubbler is perfectly clean, the resin will have a hard time finding a surface to stick to, and as a result will often settle on top of the water, resulting in the cannabis equivalent of gnarly-looking pond scum.

CARVE YOUR OWN

The mainstreaming of cannabis means that new and advanced methods of smoking are coming to market all the time, but what about those situations where you have to make do with whatever's at hand? One wonders how many camping trips were rescued by pipes MacGyvered out of a potato, a pack of Starbursts, or a cured salami. All you need in a foodstuff is something dense, carvable, and palatable—to some extent, the flavors are going to come through. The most notable such creation is probably the apple pipe, which we'll gladly walk you through.

CLASSIC APPLE PIPE

STEP 1 · CHOOSE YOUR APPLE

Find something firm and crisp; mealy fruit can give out when it comes time to creating air passages. The bigger the divot at the stem end, the better—it will serve as your bowl. You'll also need a pen, a screwdriver, or some other instrument for poking holes.

STEP 2 · FORM THE BOWL

Twist the stem until it breaks and, if needed, carve out a small bowl in its place. Jam your pen into the middle of the bowl—best to remove the ink cartridge first—creating a passage to the center of the apple. (Alternatively, you can use a toothpick to make fine holes within the bowl—mimicking a screen—that will flow into the eventual airway.)

STEP 3 · CREATE THE CARB

Create a second hole roughly an inch below the edge of your bowl that connects with your initial passage. This will be your carb. Blow into the hole to remove any stray bits of apple.

STEP 4 · AND NOW THE MOUTHPIECE

With your thumb over the carb, hold the apple to your lips and determine the most comfortable position for a mouthpiece. There you'll create a third passage that connects to the chamber. Again, blow into the hole.

STEP 5 · KEEP IT DRY

Using a lighter or matches, burn out the inside of the bowl in order to seal it as much as possible. This will limit the amount of moisture transference from the apple to your flower.

STEP 6 · LIGHT IT UP

Place your flower in the bowl and smoke it just like you would with a classic pipe!

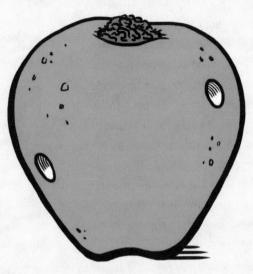

THE GRAVITY BONG

When it comes to bang for your buck, it's hard to beat the gravity bong—both in terms of the materials and the efficiency of the high. All you need is an empty 2-liter bottle, a larger container of water (a bucket or sink will do, but if you're smoking by the lakeside, use what nature has provided), and a little bit of tinfoil—though, if you can substitute a glass or metal bowl for the latter, your lungs will certainly thank you; tinfoil fumes are not exactly good for you.

STEP 1 **PREPARE YOUR BOTTLE**

Cut the bottom third from the bottle and discard it.

STEP 2 **CREATE YOUR BOWL**

If you're using glass or metal, punch a hole in the plastic cap large enough to insert the bottom of your bowl (you can seal the plastic around it with a lighter . . . just don't burn your fingers). If you're using tinfoil, remove the cap entirely and create a bowl in the bottle's open mouthpiece, pressing the edges of the foil around the outside to seal. Using a toothpick, paper clip, or pen, poke a few holes in the foil to let the smoke through.

STEP 3 **TURN ON THE FAUCET**

Fill your secondary vessel with water—it'll need to be at least 6 inches deep.

STEP 4 **SUBMERGE THE BOTTLE**

Place the open end of your bottle into the water, pushing it down until you have about 2 inches of air between your bowl and the waterline. (Be careful not to let the water into your bowl.) Once the bottle is in place, fill the bowl with ground flower.

STEP 5 **FILL THE CHAMBER**

While lighting the flower slowly lift your bottle and watch it fill with smoke. Do not remove it from the water entirely—that's what keeps the smoke from escaping.

STEP 6 **TAKE A HIT**

When your bottle is full of smoke, remove the cap or foil bowl, place your mouth over the opening, and inhale while slowly pushing the bottle back into the water and displacing the smoke. (Don't feel bad if you cough; this kind of efficiency comes with some intensity.)

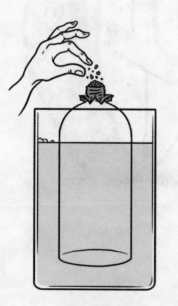
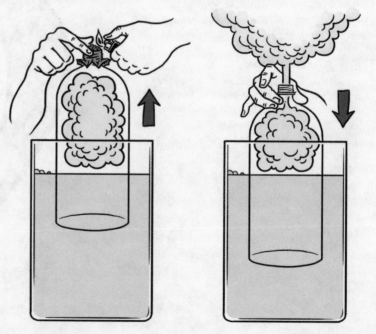

Vaporize It

Lately, at the end of a long day in the grow room, we've gravitated toward our vaporizer. It's easier on the lungs than smoking, and while long-term effects are still being studied, so far all signs point to vaping as a safer, healthier alternative. Instead of igniting the cannabis, a vaporizer heats it to just below the point of combustion. The vapor is emitted at lower temperatures—anywhere from 260 to 440°F, depending on your device's settings—activating the cannabinoids without subjecting you to the same level of tars and carcinogens.

Vaping also provides a more articulate flavor profile, since the temperature of an open flame destroys many of the delicate terpenes. You tend to get a lot more out of your cannabis when you vaporize it, since the flower only heats up as you pull; when you're smoking, it keeps smoldering as long as it's ignited. Some studies have shown—and common sense tells us—that significantly more cannabinoids are converted into usable form when vaporized.

If discretion is a priority, you'll be pleased to hear that vaporizers save you the billows of smoke and put off much less secondhand odor. They run the gamut from handheld objects that might be mistaken for a new Apple product to tabletop equipment that could sit next to your Vitamix. The biggest divide—the decision you'll have to make—is between using concentrate or flower. Some devices are built for both, but be sure to read the reviews: many of the jack-of-all-trade vaporizers tend to be masters of none. In every category there is a broad range of prices—you needn't blow your whole paycheck, but it's worth springing for quality, whichever way you go.

FLOWER-BASED VAPORIZERS

If you're growing your own, this is probably the most efficient method for you. Once your flower is cured, you'll grind it and pop it right into the chamber. (And if you're still getting the hang of drying and curing, vaporizers are far more forgiving than joints, pipes, and bongs.)

Each make and model operates a little bit differently. Some are charged with a USB cord, some with disposable batteries, and some tabletop units plug directly into a wall socket. Conduction-style devices—like the Pax—work best when the chamber is full and the flower is finely ground and evenly packed; this helps with even heat distribution. Convection-style devices—like the Firefly or the Volcano—operate best with loosely packed flower.

Tabletop devices typically offer the most precision and temperature control, but you're limited in where you can use them. Some use a hose or straw as a mouthpiece; some inflate a detachable balloon. Portable vaporizers may not have quite the power or range of a stationary device, but they certainly have the advantage in terms of convenience and portability. Either way, in most cases, you'll simply press a button, wait for a light to tell you that

11

your flower has been properly heated, then put your lips to the mouthpiece and inhale. With so many options on the market, and technology always changing, it's best to follow the manufacturer's instructions.

CONCENTRATE VAPORIZERS

Even more discreet than the flower-based versions, concentrate vaporizers are usually small, pen-shaped, and operate much like an e-cigarette. Pen vaporizers have two main components: the battery and the heating element/vessel. The style of battery usually dictates your options for the latter: oil cartridges or refillable atomizers. This isn't to say there aren't products that go against the grain—and we're hopeful that more are on the horizon—but in most cases, once you make your purchase, you'll be locked in to what kinds of concentrates and accessories are available to you. It's important to choose a model that fits your preference, so to help you make that choice, here's a primer on the two main camps.

Cartridges are either prefilled, single-use containers or reusable units you typically refill with a syringe. While they're cost-effective and convenient, we'll offer a few qualifications. Many cartridges contain additives or fillers to help the concentrate remain fluid; these fillers can leave you with a waxy, filmy mouthfeel. Perhaps more importantly, we can't speak to the long-term health effects of ingesting vaporized propylene glycol, vegetable glycerin, or even MCT oil. There are cartridges that contain no additives, but these are typically filled with BHO, RSO, or other concentrates that require a final purge to rid them of any solvents remaining from the extraction process and to strip out any extraneous plant waxes and lipids. These purges likewise strip the concentrate of its more sensitive cannabinoid and terpene components. The other asterisk that comes with cartridges is their tendency to leak. We caution against storing them on their sides or tossing them into your bag without a carrying case (especially in warmer weather).

We prefer concentrate vaporizers with refillable atomizers. The most straightforward of these is a basic bowl or chamber—usually made from quartz or ceramic—that you fill with a small dollop of concentrate. Titanium coils wrap around ceramic or quartz rods, which evenly heat the chamber and dispense the vapor. There are coil-less varieties as well—which seem to make for a less messy filling scenario, as the bowls are often deeper—but either endeavor requires a little care. If you're going this route, you'll probably want a dab tool (little metal rods that look like something your manicurist or dentist would use) to scoop out a bit of concentrate. Less is more in our experience—a lentil- to pea-sized dollop will usually do, depending on the strength of the concentrate and your own constitution—but start with less than you think you need, and learn how much you typically use in each session: overfilling will leave the inside of your pen sticky and messy. Even the most meticulous care will likely leave you with a messy device over time. Buying an additional atomizer to allow for the easy swapping of strains is helpful. Make sure to replace your atomizers as per the manufacturer's recommendations.

PEN VAPORIZORS

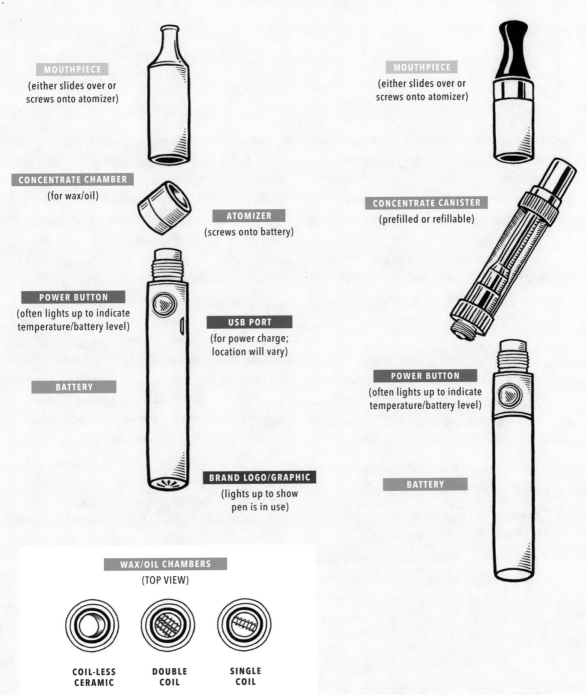

MOUTHPIECE
(either slides over or screws onto atomizer)

CONCENTRATE CHAMBER
(for wax/oil)

ATOMIZER
(screws onto battery)

POWER BUTTON
(often lights up to indicate temperature/battery level)

USB PORT
(for power charge; location will vary)

BATTERY

BRAND LOGO/GRAPHIC
(lights up to show pen is in use)

MOUTHPIECE
(either slides over or screws onto atomizer)

CONCENTRATE CANISTER
(prefilled or refillable)

POWER BUTTON
(often lights up to indicate temperature/battery level)

BATTERY

WAX/OIL CHAMBERS
(TOP VIEW)

COIL-LESS CERAMIC

DOUBLE COIL

SINGLE COIL

Dab It

Dabbing—not to be confused with Cam Newton's end-zone dance, now probably a staple of your drunk uncle's wedding repertoire—is an extremely potent method of vaporizing butane or CO_2 hash oil (also known as wax or shatter, and discussed in detail in the previous chapter). At its most basic level, dabbing involves flash vaporizing your concentrate on a hot surface and inhaling the fumes—it's like the Cadillac version of hot knives.

A dab rig can be purchased as a whole or pieced together. But the typical setup includes:

- A water pipe

- A nail—usually titanium—that fits securely into the pipe's downstem

- A glass dome that surrounds the nail, trapping the vapor before it's inhaled

- A blowtorch (a crème brûlée torch will do, but many dabbers prefer something bigger)*

- A dab tool, which looks something like a dental pick and helps you apply the concentrate to the nail

    * Alternatively, you can skip the blowtorch and opt for an e-nail, which allows you more control of the temperature and helps you to avoid inhaling butane and carbon monoxide. Unsurprisingly, this equipment will cost you.

To take a dab hit, start by applying the blowtorch's flame directly to the nail; if you're using titanium, it will eventually turn red. When it gets to that point, allow the nail to cool for 20 to 30 seconds. Using your dab tool, pick out a tiny piece of concentrate—strengths vary, but your dose shouldn't be much bigger than a bread crumb—and place it on the nail while drawing air through the mouthpiece. As soon as the concentrate stops bubbling, place your dome over the nail. Once the vapor has accumulated, remove the dome and clear the chamber as you would a bong.

Keep in mind that THC vaporizes at about 390°F, and the highest point of volatility for a chemical compound in cannabis is right around 490°F—well below the the temperature of a red-hot nail. Ideally, your nail would be heated somewhere between 400°F and 450°F. If you watch dabbing demonstrations online, you'll see plenty of young men proudly dabbing at extreme temperatures; not only are they hurting their lungs, but they're diminishing the benefits of the cannabinoids and the flavors of the concentrate.

DAB RIG

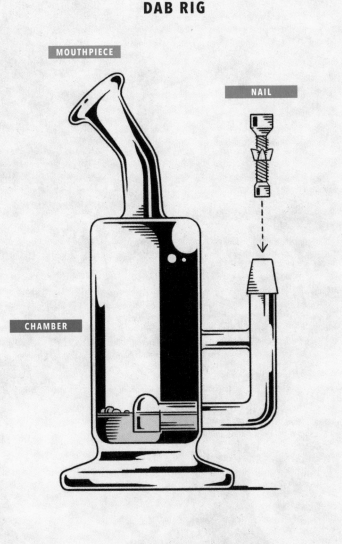

MOUTHPIECE

NAIL

CHAMBER

DAB TOOL

A FEW WORDS OF WARNING:

- Dabbing is hard on your lungs due to the high temperature and—depending on your concentrate—unsavory chemical contaminants.

- Since both the concentrate and the method are exceedingly potent—we're talking as high as 90% THC—it's more difficult to dose when dabbing. And while overdosing isn't thought to be fatal, it's *far* from pleasant.

- Likewise, breathing in high levels of butane is *far* from healthy. The standards and regulation for wax production leave room for error, so it's crucial to find a reputable producer. We favor CO_2 concentrates and prefer to avoid butane and other hydrocarbon-based extractions entirely.

- Intoxicants and a powerful blowtorch are not the most natural of friends. If you do choose to dab, use extreme caution.

- Last, and most importantly, do not attempt butane extraction at home. While we're emphatic believers in a DIY mentality, some things should be left to the professionals. There have been too many house fires and explosions for us to advocate making your own.

Chapter Twelve

COOKING WITH CANNABIS

AS WITH ALL CULINARY PURSUITS, THERE'S BOTH AN ART AND A SCIENCE TO cooking with cannabis. Not only is there the matter of complimenting the plant's natural flavors (or masking it, depending on your tastes), but also the crucial question of how you'll feel an hour or so after eating. For guidance, we've turned to the experts.

Spot, the celebrated Seattle-based edibles producer, makes some of our very favorite infused goodies, and the cannabis they use is grown with the kind of organic methods we've been preaching throughout the book. Their team of chefs and chocolatiers have worked in some of the top restaurants in the Northwest, and the Spot Brownie—their most storied creation—was already winning awards back when cannabis brands, scaled production facilities, and accurate dosing were a mere twinkle in our (slightly reddened) eyes. So you can imagine our excitement when they agreed to provide a few of their favorite recipes and to walk us through a basic infusion that will allow you to experiment with all of your own favorite baked goods. And while Spot can't offer gas chromatography analysis for each of your individual treats, they've laid out a few rules of thumb to help you infuse your home-baked edibles with more confidence and care.

Potency & Dosing

There's a common narrative among people trying edibles for the first time: they take what seems like a reasonable dose and then, after half an hour—when they still feel stone sober—they double down. Soon their heart rate is up, their breathing feels labored, and they're starting to feel dizzy. When cannabinoids enter your bloodstream through your stomach and intestines, the process is slower than when they enter through your lungs, but when the high does come on, it can be powerful and long-lasting.

Assessing the strength of your edibles goes a long way toward a more pleasant experience. But before we get to the instructions on how to do so, a quick disclaimer: unless you have access to expensive laboratory equipment, gauging potency will always rely on approximation. The strength of an infusion can vary widely depending on the plant material and success of your extraction. In addition to these variables, tolerances are unique to each person, which is why we always recommend starting slow. When coming to understand your preferred dose, start low and don't cook with your butter or oil until you know how much you need for your desired effect. And if you are an individual with a particularly high tolerance, be mindful of that fact when offering to share your goodies.

With all that said, while you may not be able to account for every variable, and you may not be able to determine potency with the same precision as a professional lab, there is a formula for calculating a cannabis infusion's THC content. But before you can begin your calculations, you need an idea of the raw materials you're working with.

- If you're using commercially grown (and thus lab-tested) cannabis, you have the number right in front of you. If the package says, simply, 21% THC, you can plug that figure into the formula below.

- If the test results contain both THC and THC-A (a label might read: "2.5% THC and 17.3% THC-A"), you first need to combine these two figures into a total THC number. Since a small amount of molecular mass is lost during the decarbing process, use the following formula first: (THC-A x .088) + THC = Total THC

- If you're using homegrown bud, or bud that came with no test results, you will have to make some assumptions based on the strain. It's hardly scientific, but when cooking with most modern hybrids, we typically estimate something in the neighborhood of 18% total THC.

- If you're using trim from homegrown cannabis, your total THC levels will be lower. We usually figure somewhere around 10%.

As with ibuprofen or caffeine, THC is measured in milligrams (mg). Since cannabis itself is typically measured in grams, you first take the dry weight and multiply by 1,000. Next, multiply that figure by the total THC as a percentage of 100.

$$(\text{Dry Weight of Cannabis in Grams} \times 1{,}000)$$
$$\times$$
$$(\text{Total THC} / 100)$$
$$= \text{Maximum Available THC}$$

There is a bit of loss in extraction efficiency with any method, but for the sake of not bogging you down with too much complicated math and measurement, and to err on the side of safety, our formula doesn't account for such losses. So, if you're working with 7 grams of cannabis (as per our instructions on page 193) with 18% total THC, the equation would shake out to:

$$(7 \times 1{,}000) \times (18/100)$$
$$= 7{,}000 \times 0.18$$
$$= 1{,}260 \text{ mg THC}$$

The infusion on page 193 calls for 1 cup of oil or butter for 7 grams of cannabis. If you're working with 1,260mg of THC, and since there are 48 teaspoons per cup, you can assume each teaspoon contains roughly 26.25 mg of THC per teaspoon.

Before you get into the kitchen and put your infusion to good use, start by sampling ¼ teaspoon (and wait 3 hours before trying more). Go up in increments of ¼ teaspoon until you've found the dose that feels right for you. This becomes your *golden number*, and we recommend writing it directly on the infusion's container.

FOR EXAMPLE: Micah likes half a teaspoon and Nichole prefers a full one. When it comes time to cook, take the number of units in a batch (say: 12 cookies) and multiply it by your golden number. Micah would want 6 teaspoons of infused butter or oil; Nichole would want 12.

Decarbing

The standout students—you who paid attention back in Chapter Two—will remember that in raw cannabis THC is stored in a nonpsychoactive form called THC-A. This molecule has an extra acid chain called a *carboxy group* that renders it useless to your CB1 receptor and thus keeps you from that high you're probably looking for. When you smoke cannabis, igniting the plant material with a flame, the THC-A undergoes a process called decarboxylation; the extra carbon atom is removed and THC-A is converted into the psychoactive THC. When cooking with cannabis, in order to unlock the THC and get the most out of your edible experience, you'll likewise need to "decarb" the plant material.

The chemists among us know that every molecule has a temperature at which it becomes volatile and evaporates, so the art of decarbing means giving the plant material enough time and heat that the THC-A converts to its active form, but not so much that you start losing the THC before you have a chance to ingest it. There are several schools of thought when it comes to decarboxylation, but this one, in our experience, is foolproof.

Decarbing Cannabis

1. Preheat oven to 240°F.

2. Grind plant material to expose as much surface area as possible. This can be done with a hand grinder or with a kitchen knife on a cutting board; be aware, cannabis is both sticky and jumpy, and chopping requires care. (You will most likely end up with sticky resin on the blade of your knife; carefully scrape it off and set it aside, as it can be enjoyed later in any manner of your choosing; see Chapter Eleven for a few ideas.)

3. Spread chopped cannabis on a foil-lined cookie tray and place on the middle rack of your preheated oven. Cook for 45 minutes, stirring every 10. (**BE AWARE**: Your kitchen—and maybe your whole house—will smell like cannabis! That's the result of terpenes and other compounds in the plant material passing their point of volatility and evaporating into the room around you. We tend to think it's a good thing—a type of aromatherapy—but make sure your family members or roommates agree.)

4. Remove from oven and allow to cool. Your plant material has now converted all (or most) of its THC-A into easy-to-ingest THC.

Infusions

Once your cannabis is decarbed, you're ready for infusion. Both THC and CBD are fat-soluble. This means that, when heated, the cannabinoids will dissolve and bind to fat molecules. Butter is probably the most common agent, but coconut oil is gaining ground—and not just among vegans. Its higher level of saturated fat makes for a more efficient and potent extraction. (Pure clarified butter, also known as ghee, will produce similar results.) Of course, potency isn't the only factor in a good edible, so depending on your recipe and your preferences, you might also experiment with olive, avocado, hempseed, or grape-seed oil.

Some cooks choose to combine the decarboxylation and infusion processes, heating the raw plant material only once it's been mixed with melted butter, but we've found the two-step process to be more precise and easier to control.

Cannabis Infusion

INGREDIENTS:
1 cup butter or coconut oil
7 grams of decarbed cannabis, chopped*
1 tbsp. of sunflower lecithin**

1. In a slow cooker or double boiler (set to medium-low), melt the butter or heat the oil.

2. Add the cannabis and cook for 3 to 4 hours, stirring occasionally.

3. Keep the heat low and watch for any smoke or boil. If smoke rises, remove the mixture from heat and let it cool before resuming.

4. Using a sieve lined with cheesecloth, carefully strain the mixture into a glass container. Ring out cheesecloth to free any remaining oils.

5. Discard plant material and let oil or butter cool.

6. Clearly label your container with a suggested dose and refrigerate.

* *We advise against grinding too finely, as it will make it hard to filter out*

** *Optional, but it enhances the absorption of THC in the body; this makes your edibles more efficient, not stronger, which means you can use less butter.*

Super Gooey Brownies

by Hilary Brown

In the world of edibles, nothing is so iconic, so tried and true, as the pot brownie. Even Alice B. Toklas couldn't resist wedging some variation—more of a fudge—into her famous, eponymous cookbook. "Euphoria and brilliant storms of laughter," Toklas promised. "Ecstatic reveries and extensions of one's personality on several simultaneous planes are to be complacently expected." Hear, hear! On top of that, the cannabis flavor just blends well with dark chocolate. But too often, cannabis brownies are of the store-bought, add-an-egg variety. Why settle when you can bake a dessert that provides a little euphoria of its own?

Before you start cooking, best to review our section on potency and dosing (see pages 190–191) and establish your golden number. Once you know your perfect dosage, multiply by 12, and substitute that quantity of infused butter for a portion of the butter below.

1. Preheat oven to 350°F.

2. Place both the non-infused butter and cannabis butter in the bowl of a stand mixer fitted with the paddle attachment.

3. Cream the butter at a low speed until it is smooth with no visible lumps.

4. In the meantime, melt the chocolate in a double boiler—or in a metal bowl perched on a saucepan with roughly an inch of boiling water—until warm. Stir often during the melting process in order to prevent scorching.

5. With the mixer still set to low, slowly drizzle the melted chocolate into the butter.

6. As soon as the chocolate is incorporated, stop the mixer and scrape the sides of the bowl with a rubber spatula.

7. Return to low speed, add both varieties of sugar and the cocoa powder, and mix until all ingredients are incorporated.

8. Stop the mixer and scrape the sides of the bowl with a rubber spatula, making sure there are no lumps of sugar or cocoa powder.

9. Return the mixer to low speed, then slowly add the vanilla extract and eggs—one at a time, scraping between each addition.

10. As soon as the eggs are fully incorporated, add the flour, salt, and baking soda. Mix just to combine (you do not want to overmix at this point).

11. Pour batter into a greased 8" square pan, spreading it evenly with a rubber spatula, and bake for 35 to 40 minutes. The top of the brownies should be slightly puffy.

12. Remove the pan from the oven and allow brownies to cool on a rack before cutting. (This is crucial due to the gooey texture.)

YIELD: 12 brownies

INGREDIENTS:

¾ cup unsalted butter
(see above)

4 oz. 100% cacao baking chocolate, finely chopped*

1½ cups pure cane sugar

¾ cup loosely packed brown sugar

½ cup Dutch-process unsweetened cocoa powder

1 tsp. vanilla extract

3 large eggs

¾ cup all-purpose flour

¼ tsp. kosher salt

¼ tsp. baking soda

* We've had great results with Dagoba and Scharffen Berger bars

Quoc's Cornbread

by Quoc

Not everyone has such a sweet tooth. Just because you prefer a savory snack to a sugary one, it doesn't mean you should have to forgo that deep body high that edibles can offer. And considering what cannabis can do for your appetite and enjoyment of food, doesn't it make a certain kind of sense to infuse the appetizer course?

Once again, before you start measuring out your ingredients, we recommend reviewing our section on potency and dosing (see pages 190–191) and establishing your golden number. When you know your perfect dosage, multiply by 9, and substitute that quantity of infused butter for a portion of the butter below.

1. Preheat the oven to 370°F.

2. Place the non-infused butter into a medium heavy-bottomed saucepan over medium heat. Set aside the infused portion in a small bowl (preferably metal, as it will cool faster).

3. Once the butter has completely melted, add the corn kernels and continue to cook until the butter begins to brown, about 10 to 15 minutes. The butter will start to form brown specks as the fat separates from the water—the more specks, the deeper the flavor. Remove immediately from heat, scrape the bottom of the pan—you want to release those delicious brown bits—and pour over the cannabis butter. Allow to cool to room temperature.

4. Combine the heavy cream, whole milk, corn syrup, sugar, and egg in a blender and purée at high speed for 30 seconds. The egg should break down and become indistinguishable from the other ingredients, and the whole mixture should be smooth.

5. Once the corn-butter mixture has cooled, add it to the blender and purée at high speed until it's smooth, about 2 to 3 minutes.

6. In a large metal bowl, combine $1/3$ cup of the cornmeal with the remaining dry ingredients and slowly pour the liquid ingredients over the top, stirring with a rubber spatula for about 5 minutes. Make sure there are no pockets of dry ingredients. You can opt to use a stand mixer, but it will make for a slightly tougher product in the end. If you choose to add bacon, chilies, freeze-dried corn, or cheese, now is the moment to fold them into your batter, stirring gently.

7. Grease the bottom and sides of an 8" square pan and sprinkle with the remaining cornmeal. A thin dusting should stick, and the rest can be tapped out and discarded. This layer creates a bit of a barrier and allows the cornbread to easily release from the pan.

8. Pour in the batter, spreading it evenly with a rubber spatula, and bake for 25 minutes.

9. Allow to cool 5 to 10 minutes before cutting into 9 equal squares.

10. Serve warm with butter, salt, and honey.

YIELD: 9 pieces

INGREDIENTS:

½ cup unsalted butter
  (see above)

1½ cups frozen corn kernels

3 tbsp. heavy cream

2 tbsp. whole milk

2 tbsp. corn syrup

1 large egg

½ cup cornmeal, medium
  grind (divided)

½ cup all-purpose flour

1½ tbsp. pure cane sugar

½ tsp. kosher salt

½ tsp. baking powder

⅛ tsp. baking soda

OPTIONAL:

2 tbsp. ground freeze-
  dried corn

5 pieces of crisp bacon,
  chopped into ½-inch
  pieces

½ cup diced green chilies

½ cup shredded cheddar
  cheese

Salt, butter, and/or honey for
  serving

Chocolate Shell

by Hilary Brown

If cannabis tends to send you on a nostalgia kick, maybe you'll go for an updated and upgraded version of Magic Shell—that quick-hardening chocolate sauce you may remember from the dip cones of your youth. It's quick, easy, and adds a little variety to the ice cream in your freezer. Pour it over a scoop or two and enjoy the rich flavor and extra dimension of texture.

Other than the chocolate itself, coconut oil is the principal ingredient here. If that's your infusion of choice, just swap in cannabis coconut oil for the oil listed below. You can substitute the full amount or a portion of it; for the latter, calculate your golden number (see pages 190–191) and multiply by 10. If you're working with a butter infusion, you can replace up to 1 tablespoon of the coconut oil with cannabis butter. We prefer full coconut oil; butter tends to soften and it slightly delays the hardening reaction, but if that's all you've got, we'll wager that you won't hear any complaints.

1. Melt the chocolate in a double boiler—or in a metal bowl perched on a saucepan with roughly an inch of boiling water—stirring regularly until warm and completely melted. Take care not to exceed 125°F.

2. Remove from heat and immediately add the coconut oil and/or butter (both infused and non-infused portions) and stir to combine. These ingredients should melt into the chocolate at 100°F within 5 minutes. If 5 minutes have passed and the butter has not fully melted, place the bowl back over boiling water and allow to heat for about 15 seconds at a time, stirring in between, until you have a smooth, even mixture.

3. Allow to cool slightly. The chocolate mixture should be able to drop to 75°F without solidifying, but keep an eye on the texture. If you notice it beginning to harden, reintroduce low heat.

4. Pour over ice cream or dip your favorite frozen treat into the chocolate shell.

5. Sauce will keep at room temperature for 2 weeks in a clean, dry container. (Heatproof glass, such as a wide-mouth canning jar, is ideal.) To reheat, place the whole container in a pot of warm water; make sure the lid is well above the surface, as water and chocolate don't mix. Heat on low for about 5 minutes. Sauce should be pourable, but not hot—about 75°F.

YIELD: 1¼ cup
(about 10 servings)

INGREDIENTS:

8 oz. dark chocolate, 70% cacao or higher *

4 tbsp. 100% coconut oil
(see above)

OPTIONAL

1 tbsp. unsalted butter
(see above)

* You can play to your own personal palate here, but we've had great results with Scharffen Berger, Green and Black's, and Endangered Species bars. Avoid chocolate chips, as they typically contain extra stabilizers that will affect the desired consistency.

Glossary

420: While there are competing theories about the origin of this term, the most common traces it back to a group of San Rafael high school students in the seventies. They met each afternoon at 4:20 to search the woods for an abandoned grow operation and, eventually, the time became their code word. Some suggest it was a police code for cannabis, overheard—and quickly coopted—by stoners. Whatever its origin, 420 has become an all-purpose shorthand for cannabis-friendly people and places and 4/20 (April 20th) has become a "high holiday."

AEROBIC: The term used for microorganisms that require oxygen. In aerobic composting, aerating your pile (by turning or tumbling its contents) will provide aerobic organisms with the oxygen they need to decompose plant matter. **CHAPTER SIX**

AEROPONICS: A system of delivering nutrients to plants by misting their air-suspended roots. **CHAPTER SIX**

ANAEROBIC: The term used for microorganisms that do not require oxygen. While there *are* methods of anaerobic composting, in the system we describe, anaerobic activity—usually identified by the putrid smell—is an indication of harmful bacteria. **CHAPTER SIX**

AMSTERDAM: The capital city of cannabis. The Netherlands began its legalization efforts in 1976, and has been a tourist destination for growers and enthusiasts ever since. **CHAPTER ONE**

AUTOFLOWERING STRAIN: A plant that grows and flowers without regard to light and temperature cues. **CHAPTER SEVEN**

BALLAST: A device that regulates electrical current before it reaches your light fixture. **CHAPTER THREE**

BHANG: Cannabis leaves and flower ground into a fine paste and usually consumed as a beverage made with milk, ghee, and spices. In India, bhang is commonly consumed during religious festivals, such as Holi and Shivaratri.

BHO (BUTANE HASH OIL): This concentrate comes in a variety of forms and can be used—depending on its consistency—in vaporizers or dab rigs. It's popular for its high levels of THC, but can be dangerous to produce and to consume. **CHAPTER TEN**

BIOCHAR: A specialized form of charcoal usually produced from plant matter. As a soil amendment, it helps with water retention and the moderation of acidity, and aids in cultivating beneficial microorganisms. **CHAPTER SIX**

BLACK MARKET: The buying and selling of cannabis outside of licensed recreational shops and medical dispensaries.

BLUE LIGHT: The portion of the visible light spectrum dominant in the spring and early summer. Plants—both in nature and in the grow room—use blue light for vegetative growth.

BLUNT: A joint rolled with the tobacco-leaf wrapper of a cigar. **CHAPTER ELEVEN**

BONG: A popular form of water pipe made up of a water chamber, a tube, a downstem, and a bowl. **CHAPTER ELEVEN**

BOTRYTIS: Also known as bud rot (or noble rot in winemaking circles), this gray mold starts as an innocuous film on a plant's flowers and leaves, but can quickly wipe out a crop. **CHAPTER EIGHT**

BUD: Another term for the cannabis flower, and home to the highest concentration of resin-rich trichomes. **CHAPTER TWO**

BUDTENDER: Your friendly neighborhood cannabis salesperson. If you're lucky, they will walk you through each strain's characteristics and flavor profile to help you make an informed purchase.

CALYX: The tear-shaped nodules present in the flower that contain the plant's reproductive material. **CHAPTER TWO**

CANNABACEAE: The plant family that cannabis shares with hops, nettle trees, and many ornamental plants. **CHAPTER TWO**

CANNABINOID: The chemical compounds, which, when received by cannabinoid receptors in the brain and nervous system, are responsible for the wide array of cannabis's physical and mental effects. The two most well-known cannabinoids are THC and CBD. **CHAPTER TWO**

CANNABIS CUP: The most prestigious cannabis competition and trade show in the world, hosted by *High Times* magazine. **CHAPTER ONE**

CARBON DIOXIDE (CO$_2$): A colorless, tasteless, odorless gas necessary for photosynthesis. Carbon dioxide is also used to extract concentrates. (We strongly prefer it to butane.) **CHAPTER THREE; CHAPTER TEN**

CARBON FILTER: A device that, through the chemical process of adsorption, helps purify the air of odor and contaminants. **CHAPTER THREE**

CBD (CANNABIDIOL): One of the primary cannabinoids found in cannabis, CBD is nonpsychoactive, but is largely responsible for many of the plant's physical benefits. It also lessens some of THC's psychoactive effects. **CHAPTER TWO**

CBN (CANNABINOL): Broadly speaking, this cannabinoid is the end result of aged or oxidized THC; it's still psychoactive to some degree, but is known for its sedative effects. **CHAPTER TWO**

CERAMIC METAL HALIDE: A variety of metal-halide lamp that uses a ceramic arc rather than quartz. **CHAPTER THREE**

CEREBRAL: A common descriptor for a more psychoactive high (often referred to as "heady"). This effect is usually associated with sativa-dominant strains, though it's certainly not exclusive to them. **CHAPTER TWO**

CFM (CUBIC FEET PER MINUTE): A unit of measurement for air velocity, and how you'll determine the power of a fan or ventilation system. **CHAPTER THREE**

CHELATED NUTRIENTS: Nutrients that are bonded to an organic material—or ligand—that allows plants to absorb them. (*Chelate* comes from the Greek word for "claw".) **CHAPTER SIX**

CHLOROPHYLL: The chemical, found in a plant cell's chloroplasts, that enables photosynthesis. **CHAPTER SEVEN**

CHRONIC: Snoop Dogg claims to have coined the term after mishearing someone refer to "hydroponics." He started using the word to describe any good, potent cannabis, and it quickly caught on with other rappers (including, of course, Dr. Dre). **CHAPTER ONE**

CLAY: The finest of soil's principal particles. **CHAPTER SIX**

CLONE: A cutting taken from another plant, then rooted and cultivated on its own. Clones have the exact same genetics as their mother plant. **CHAPTER SEVEN**

COFFEE SHOP: Not to be confused with regular old cafés, Amsterdam's "coffee shops" are licensed to sell cannabis, and customers are allowed to enjoy it on the premises.

COLA: A bud site, or cluster of flowers, on a female cannabis plant. **CHAPTER TWO**

COMPOST: A high-nutrient amalgam of decayed organic material; very useful in living soil. **CHAPTER SIX**

COMPOST TEA: An aerated, water-based compost concentrate that can help to expand the diversity and abundance of microorganisms in soil. **CHAPTER SIX**

CONCENTRATE: A catch-all term for the oils, waxes, and tinctures that are made by extracting cannabinoids from the cannabis plant. **CHAPTER TEN**

COTTONMOUTH: A common side effect of cannabis. The human mouth has cannabinoid receptors in its saliva-producing glands, and certain cannabinoids delay commands between these glands and the nervous system. This results in low saliva and a dry mouth. Nothing to be concerned about: just grab something to drink or suck on a piece of hard candy.

COUCH-LOCK: Have you ever smoked a strong indica joint and felt too stoned to move? That's couch-lock. People use the term to characterize the effects of potent, heavy-CBN strains. **CHAPTER TWO**

CURE: The process of slowly drying cannabis for better flavors and a smoother smoke. **CHAPTER NINE**

D-LIMONENE: A citrusy terpene commonly found in cannabis. D-limonene is a highly effective natural cleaning solution, and particularly great for getting that sticky resin off your hands and tools. **CHAPTER TWO; CHAPTER SIX**

DAB/DABBING: A potent method of vaporizing cannabis concentrate, using butane combustion and a special "dab rig." **CHAPTER ELEVEN**

DANK: This term was originally used to describe a strain's overpowering aroma, but the cannabis bros have expanded the definition; it's now used to describe any particularly potent bud.

DECARBOXYLATION/DECARB: The process of converting THC-A and CBD-A into activated THC and CBD. This is typically accomplished with heat. **CHAPTER TWELVE**

DEHUMIDIFIER: An appliance that pulls moisture from the air and helps to regulate humidity levels. **CHAPTER FOUR**

DISPENSARY: A licensed distributor of medical cannabis. Unlike a recreational shop, one must have a doctor's prescription or medical card to patronize these businesses. **CHAPTER ONE**

DITCH WEED: A loose term for subpar cannabis—low potency, unpleasant flavors, unknown origins.

EDIBLE: While baked goods may dominate the landscape, any cannabis-infused food or beverage falls into the category of edible. ("Medible" is the term used for products produced and distributed for medical purposes, and they're a popular alternative for patients who prefer not to smoke or vape.) **CHAPTER TWELVE**

ENDO: Another slang term for cannabis, popularized by Snoop Dogg, Nas, and others. Some speculate that it originally referred to cannabis grown indoors—which was assumed to be strong stuff—but now it's used more broadly.

ENTOURAGE EFFECT: The interaction of cannabis's various compounds—cannabinoids and terpenes—that can boost, block, and otherwise affect the physical and mental properties of cannabis. This is largely why synthetic THC doesn't have the same impact. **CHAPTER TWO**

FAN LEAVES: The large (and iconic) cannabis leaves that are key players in photosynthesis and transpiration. Since fan leaves contain very few trichomes, they're typically discarded after harvest. **CHAPTER TWO**

FEMINIZED: Seeds that have been bred to produce only female plants. **CHAPTER SEVEN**

FLOWER: Also known as "buds," these clusters of blossoms on female cannabis plants are the raison d'être of growing. They're what you'll eventually harvest, cure, and smoke, as they contain the highest concentration of trichomes on the plant. **CHAPTER TWO**

FLOWERING GROWTH: The stage of a plant's life cycle when it stops putting energy toward vegetative growth and starts developing flowers and reproductive material. **CHAPTER SEVEN**

FLUORESCENT: A tube-shaped lamp that uses mercury vapor and phosphor coating to produce visible light. The phosphor coating can be optimized for particular color spectrums, which are useful for various stages of plant development. **CHAPTER THREE**

FOLIAR APPLICATION: The process of feeding your plants nutrients by misting their leaves. **CHAPTER SEVEN**

FOUR-FINGER BAG: Old-school slang for roughly an ounce of cannabis. In the seventies, if a sandwich baggie was full to four fingers, it'd run you about $10. (Sigh . . . simpler times.)

GANJA: A slang term derived from the Hindi word for cannabis: *gãjā*.

GRASS: Yet another slang term for cannabis.

GRAVITY BONG: A homemade smoking device, easily assembled from a plastic bottle and bucket. About as economical a high as you can find, but—all too often—a bit overpowering. (See Season Three, Episode Six of HBO's excellent *High Maintenance*.) **CHAPTER ELEVEN**

GRINDER: A small handheld instrument that breaks your flower down into easily rollable pieces. The best ones screen and store any kief lost in the grinding process. **CHAPTER ELEVEN**

HASH/HASHISH: A compressed resin made from kief (or loose resin glands), which, typically, has been sifted or washed from the cannabis flower. Hash can be smoked, vaporized, or used in cooking. **CHAPTER TEN**

HASH OIL: Also known as budder, shatter, honeycomb, or wax—mostly depending on the texture. Hash oil is a cannabis concentrate produced with solvent-based extraction, such as butane or CO_2. **CHAPTER TEN**

HEMP: Low-THC cannabis strains cultivated mostly for their fiber and oil. **CHAPTER TWO**

HID (HIGH INTENSITY DISCHARGE): The category of lighting that includes metal halide and high pressure sodium—both are popular options for indoor growing. **CHAPTER THREE**

HIGH-PRESSURE SODIUM: A variety of gas discharge lamp. Because their light spectrum peaks in the 500–700nm range, they're best used for flowering growth. **CHAPTER THREE**

HIGH TIMES: The most influential and well-known cannabis publication. Founded in 1974, *High Times* has published such legends as Hunter S. Thompson, Truman Capote, William S. Burroughs—and even an interview with Susan Sontag. The magazine is also responsible for the Cannabis Cup. **CHAPTER ONE**

HYDROPONICS: A system of growing cannabis in which the plant's roots are supported by an inert medium and given a highly controlled formula of liquids or powdered nutrients. **CHAPTER SIX**

INDICA: One of the two primary subspecies of cannabis. While indica-dominant strains vary widely in their effects and characteristics, they're commonly known for strong, relaxing body highs. **CHAPTER TWO**

IN-LINE FAN: A fan that connects to ducting or ventilation and is used to pull air from one space into another. **CHAPTER THREE**

ISO: This concentrate uses isopropyl alcohol to separate trichomes from the plant material. **CHAPTER TEN**

JOINT: The classic. Ground cannabis wrapped in rolling papers. **CHAPTER ELEVEN**

KIEF: The separated resin glands (also known as trichomes) that may accumulate in your grinder or can be sifted from cannabis flower with a mesh screen or sieve. Kief is often pressed into cakes of hash, but it can also be vaporized or smoked. **CHAPTER TEN**

KUSH: While the term is often used as a synonym for good weed, this family of indica strains comes from the Hindu Kush mountain range in Pakistan and Afghanistan, and is known for producing excellent hashish. **CHAPTER TWO**

LANDRACE: A native strain of cannabis that has adapted to its local environment. Often named for their region of origin—Afghani, Thai, Hawaiian, etc.—these strains are the building blocks for all hybrids that came later. **CHAPTER TWO**

LED (LIGHT EMITTING DIODES): A highly efficient lamp which comes in a variety of light spectrums, which can be used for both vegetative and flowering growth. **CHAPTER THREE**

LID: Seventies slang for an eyeballed ounce of cannabis. Supposedly that's about what fit into the lid of a coffee canister. Some argue that the term originally referred to a tobacco can (which holds about an eighth).

LOAM: A soil made up of sand, silt, and clay. **CHAPTER SIX**

LOW-STRESS TRAINING: Any canopy-management technique that doesn't involve cutting or pruning. The goal is to manipulate branches to grow in whatever direction maximizes their exposure to light. **CHAPTER SEVEN**

LUMEN (LM): A unit of measurement for the total quantity of visible light emitted by a source. **CHAPTER THREE**

MARIJUANA: One of the most common terms for cannabis, it was popularized in the 1930s as a variant of the Spanish *marihuana* in an attempt to make the plant seem foreign and, therefore, dangerous. **CHAPTER ONE**

MEDICAL: The designation for cannabis produced, tested, and distributed exclusively for patients with prescriptions or medical cards. There are currently twenty-eight states (along with the District of Columbia) that have legalized medical cannabis. **CHAPTER ONE**

METAL HALIDE: A variety of high-intensity discharge lamp. Because their light spectrum peaks in the 400–600nm range, they're best used for vegetative growth. **CHAPTER THREE**

MICROBIOME: The community of microorganisms in living soil. **CHAPTER SIX**

MICROMOLES (µMOL): A unit of measurement for the number of photons passing through a target area. When measuring PAR, you typically calculate micromoles per square meter per second.

MOTHER: A female plant kept in vegetative growth and used for procuring clones. **CHAPTER SEVEN**

MUNCHIES: A quick-to-hit and difficult-to-sate hunger, and a common side effect of cannabis. THC can increase sensitivity in the olfactory bulb (which leads to heightened pleasure when it comes to smell and taste), but it also triggers neuropathways in the brain that regulate hunger.

NITROGEN (N): One of the three essential elements for plant growth, and key to the production of chlorophyll. **CHAPTER EIGHT**

NODE: The point on the plant's stem from which leaves, buds, and branches grow.

NORML: The National Organization for the Reform of Marijuana Laws, which was formed in 1970 in response to the Controlled Substance Act. "NORML's mission is to move public opinion sufficiently to legalize the responsible use of marijuana by adults, and to serve as an advocate for consumers to assure they have access to high quality marijuana that is safe, convenient and affordable."

NUG: Slang term for cannabis flower (or bud).

OMRI: The Organic Materials Review Institute, which provides an independent review of fertilizers, pest controls, and other inputs intended for use in certified organic production and processing. **CHAPTER SIX**

PAR (PHOTOSYNTHETICALLY ACTIVATED RADIATION): The spectrum of light—spanning 400 to 700 nanometers (nm)—that plants can use for growth. **CHAPTER THREE**

pH (POTENTIAL OF HYDROGEN): A scale of 0–14 used to specify acidity and basicity. Cannabis does best in a growing medium with near neutral pH—somewhere in the range of 6.5–8.

PHENOTYPE: The outward, observable characteristics of a plant, governed by genes as well as environmental influences. **CHAPTER TWO**

PHOSPHOROUS (P): One of the three essential elements for plant growth, and key to both root development and flowering growth. **CHAPTER EIGHT**

PHOTOPERIOD: The period of daylight in a twenty-hour cycle in which a plant receives light. **CHAPTER THREE**

PHOTOSYNTHESIS: The process by which plants capture light energy and convert it into chemical energy. **CHAPTER SEVEN**

PHOTOTROPISM: The plant's orientation in response to light; while certain organisms might grow away from a light source, cannabis always grows toward it. This is an important principal to remember when you're training your canopy. **CHAPTER SEVEN**

PISTIL: The small hairlike strands that emerge from the calyx of the female cannabis plant. The pistil's job is to capture pollen to fertilize the ovule. **CHAPTER TWO**

POLLEN SAC: The structure on male cannabis plants in which pollen is produced. **CHAPTER TWO**

POT: Yet another slang term for cannabis. This one comes from the Spanish *potiguaya* (itself an amalgamation of *potación de guaya*: "drink of grief"), a wine or brandy in which cannabis has been steeped.

PRE-ROLL: As the name suggests, these joints come rolled (or packed) for you. Convenient as they may be, they're not always filled with the highest quality cannabis, so be sure to ask your budtender for a recommendation. **CHAPTER ELEVEN**

PROPAGATION: Producing a new plant, either by seed or by clone. **CHAPTER SEVEN**

PRUNING: The act of trimming or removing leaves and branches to strengthen the whole of the plant or to allow for better exposure to light. **CHAPTER SEVEN**

PSYCHOACTIVE: A chemical, such as THC, that has a significant effect on mental processes. **CHAPTER TWO**

RECREATIONAL: The designation for legalized cannabis that can be purchased and consumed without a prescription or medical card. **CHAPTER ONE**

RED LIGHT: The portion of the visible light spectrum dominant in the late summer and fall. Plants use red light for flowering growth. **CHAPTER THREE**

REEFER: Yet another slang term for cannabis and yet another instance where English smokers borrowed Mexican argot. It's thought that "reefer" comes from the Spanish *griffa*.

RESIN: The sap-like substance found in trichomes, which contain the majority of the plant's cannabinoids. **CHAPTER TWO**

RESPIRATION: The process by which plants metabolize photosynthates and release water and carbon dioxide into the atmosphere. **CHAPTER SEVEN**

RICK SIMPSON OIL (RSO): Also known as Phoenix Tears, this concentrate is extracted with isopropyl alcohol. Its inventor—a prominent cannabis activist and the concentrate's namesake—claims it helped cure his skin cancer. **CHAPTER TEN**

ROOT: The lower portion of the plant that extends into the growing medium, taking in water and nutrients and providing structural support. **CHAPTER TWO**

ROOT APHID: Also known as grape phylloxera, these tiny insects feast on cannabis leaves and roots; an infestation can do severe damage to a crop. **CHAPTER EIGHT**

ROSIN: A cannabis concentrate produced with a mechanical process of applied heat and pressure. **CHAPTER TEN**

RUDERALIS: A lesser known, and typically wild, cannabis subspecies. **CHAPTER TWO**

SATIVA: One of the two primary subspecies of cannabis. While sativa-dominant strains vary widely in their effects and characteristics, they're commonly known for heady, energetic highs. **CHAPTER TWO**

SCHWAG: Slang for low-quality cannabis. Think brown, dry, and seedy.

SEA OF GREEN (SOG): Generally refers to the practice of fitting a large number of plants under your lights, then instigating flowering at a relatively young age. **CHAPTER SEVEN**

SEED: The embryonic form of a plant, protected by a hard outer covering. **CHAPTER SEVEN**

SHATTER: A form of concentrate that takes on a glass-like consistency. Shatter is most popular among vape and dab enthusiasts. **CHAPTER TEN**

SOIL FOOD WEB: The chain of organisms—plants, animals, fungus, and bacteria—responsible for breaking down organic matter in the soil and providing the nutrients that plants need to live. **CHAPTER SIX**

SPLIFF: A marijuana cigarette. **CHAPTER ELEVEN**

STOMATA: The small, adjustable pores on the undersides of cannabis leaves. **CHAPTER SEVEN**

STRAIN: Not to be confused with the three principal subspecies (sativa, indica, and ruderalis), this term refers to the myriad landrace and hybrid varieties of cannabis. **CHAPTER TWO**

SUBLINGUAL: Latin for "under the tongue," this is the suggested method for administering cannabis tinctures. **CHAPTER TEN**

SUGAR LEAF: The small, trichome-covered leaves growing within the cannabis flower. While they're not ideal for smoking, sugar leaves are useful for making various concentrates. **CHAPTER TWO**

SUPER CROPPING: A canopy management technique that involves reorienting growth to maximize light exposure, and strategically damaging the plant to trigger a reinforcement of the stems. **CHAPTER SEVEN**

TAPROOT: The principal downward-growing root from which all other rootlets spring forth.

TERMINAL BUD: Also known as the leader or apical bud, this is the primary bud site located at the tip of the stem. **CHAPTER TWO**

TERPENE: The essential oils that not only give cannabis its aroma and flavor, but also contribute to its physiological and psychoactive benefits. (See the entry for "Entourage Effect.") **CHAPTER TWO**

THC (TETRAHYDROCANNABINOL): Cannabis's principal psychoactive component and the most highly concentrated cannabinoid. **CHAPTER TWO**

TINCTURE: An easy-to-make, easy-to-take alcohol-based concentrate. **CHAPTER TEN**

TIPPING: A canopy-management technique in which a small cut is made at the top of a shoot, triggering the growth of two colas instead of one. **CHAPTER SEVEN**

TOPICALS: Cannabis products—such as lotions and creams—that deliver cannabinoids into the skin tissue but do not breach the bloodstream. Topicals are often used for soothing headaches and sore muscles. **CHAPTER TEN**

TOPPING: A canopy-management technique in which the terminal bud is removed in order to expose lower branches to light and to encourage more robust growth among secondary shoots. **CHAPTER SEVEN**

TRANSPIRATION: The process by which water is carried through the plants, from the roots to the stomata. **CHAPTER SEVEN**

TRANSDERMAL: Cannabis products—such as patches—that deliver cannabinoids directly into the bloodstream. **CHAPTER TEN**

TRICHOME: The mushroom-shaped, resin-filled glands found primarily on the cannabis flower. **CHAPTER TWO**

TRIM: The leaf matter left behind after trimming. While it doesn't have the same density of trichomes as bud, it contains enough that it's valuable for cooking, collecting kief or hash, and creating concentrates. **CHAPTER NINE**

TRIMMING: The act of cutting away plant material covered in fewer trichomes, so that you're left with cannabinoid-rich buds. **CHAPTER NINE**

TURGIDITY: The level of distension or swelling from fluid. Plant cells need to be sufficiently turgid to keep from wilting. **CHAPTER SEVEN**

VAPORIZER: A portable or stationary device that heats—without combusting—flower or concentrates into vapor. **CHAPTER ELEVEN**

VEGETATIVE GROWTH: The earlier stage of a plant's life cycle—after propagation but before flowering—when it devotes its energy to growing tall, bulky, and strong. **CHAPTER SEVEN**

WAX: A form of concentrate that takes on a honey-like consistency. Wax is most popular among vape and dab enthusiasts. **CHAPTER TEN**

WEED: A (particularly popular) slang term for cannabis.

Contributors

RASKAL TURBEVILLE is a mycologist and soil biologist originally from Ojai, California.

HILARY BROWN is a pastry chef and Spot's chocolatier. She has worked in the kitchens of the Alexis Hotel, Tulio's Restaurant, Columbia Tower Club, the Fairmont Olympic Hotel, and Tom Douglas's Tanakasan. She founded Restless Chocolates, worked as chocolatier for Vibrant Chocolates, and was featured in *Chocolate: The Reference Standard*. Her confections have received gold awards from the International Chocolate Salon.

QUOC is a Seattle-based chef who has cooked at Rover's, Agrodolce, Chan, Chefsteps, and Loulay, and now works for Botanica Seattle. He gets his inspirations from his geema, his friends, anime, comics, cartoons, and a burger. Quoc has trained under amazing chefs, most importantly Corina Johnson, who pushed him to strive for perfection with his weird shenanigans, switching around from sweet to savory.

ALLEN CRAWFORD is an illustrator, designer, and writer. He and his wife Susan are proprietors of the design/illustration studio Plankton Art Co. Their most notable project to date is the collection of 400 species identification illustrations that are on permanent display at the American Museum of Natural History's Milstein Hall of Ocean Life. He is the author of *Whitman Illuminated: Song of Myself* and, under his pseudonym, Lord Breaulove Swells Whimsy, he wrote, designed, and illustrated *The Affected Provincial's Companion, Volume One*, which was optioned for film by Johnny Depp's production company, Infinitum Nihil. He lives in Mt. Holly, New Jersey.

Before we acknowledge the many individuals who helped create Grow Your Own, *we want to call attention to the long-term damage of this country's foolish—and deeply racist—war on drugs. White people use cannabis at the same rate as people of color, but the latter have faced incarceration or felony charges in wildly disproportionate numbers. Even as prohibition wanes, the harm remains, including when individuals with felony convictions are barred from holding legal cannabis licenses. We'd also like to recognize The Minority Cannabis Business Association, an organization that is doing something to combat the problem. The MCBA's mission is "to create equal access and economic empowerment for cannabis businesses, their patients, and the communities most affected by the war on drugs." Not only do they provide assistance and advocacy for business owners of color, but they also work to get non-violent cannabis-related offenses expunged from individuals' criminal records, so that everyone has fair access to the opportunities created by this new industry. Visit their website at www.minoritycannabis.org*

Acknowledgments

We'd like to thank everyone that contributed their time, thoughts, advice, words, photos, illustrations, and spaces to make *Grow Your Own* what it is. Thanks to Raskal Turbeville for sharing his living-soil expertise, and to everyone at Spot—particularly Lena Davidson, Hilary Brown, and Quoc—for walking us through the process of cooking with cannabis (and providing those delectable recipes).

Thanks to Allen Crawford for sketching everything from the soil food web to a gravity bong; to Brenton Salo, Will Malzahn, Jesse Tobler, Everett Yockey, Zak Davis, and Jayson Bosteder of Juliet Zulu for the photo shoots; to Zachary Minick, Wade Preeble of Oregon Breeders Group, Marcus Richardson (aka BCBubbleman), Santiago Miguel of Quinubu Farms, Marijuana Resources, Jim Baker, Whitney Cranshaw, and Bruce Watt for additional photography. Thanks as well to Portland's Serra, for letting us shoot in their beautiful store (and sharing their lovely Summerland Ceramic Stonerware bongs), to Alela and Toren Volkmann for offering up their house and modeling our various edibles, and to Karen Hancock for lending us her hands and unmatched trimming skills.

Thanks to Steep Hill Labs for the highly informative breakdowns of cannabanoids' therapeutic properties and synthesis.

Thanks to Diane Chonette, Jakob Vala, and the whole crew at Tin House Books. And a special thanks to our editor, Tony Perez, whose patience and steady hand guided us forward as we got lost in our stoner thought spirals, and whose overarching vision tied this entire project together.

IMAGE CREDITS

NICHOLE GRAF is Raven Grass's creative director and head of product development. A designer, illustrator, fine artist, stylist, and art director by trade, she worked as a footwear and accessories designer for Madewell in NYC, before moving West. This background, combined with her deep interest in alternative medicine, nutrition, and the natural world, led her to the creation of Raven Grass and its product offerings.

DAVID STEIN is Raven Grass's master gardener. He has over forty years of experience cultivating cannabis in both Amsterdam and the United States. Known for his use of organic nutrient development and natural pest control, as well as his passion for unique strain development, Stein has been awarded "Best Weed" at *High Times*'s Cannabis Cup, first place at Highlife Hemp Fair's Hash Cup, and his exclusive strain Stella Blue was featured in Jason King's *Cannabible 3*.

MICAH SHERMAN is a trained architect who has worked in construction management, technical design for the modern luxury furniture brand Poliform, and as operations director for Hailey Development Group. His understanding of building and engineering has allowed Raven Grass to pursue innovative and uniquely effective systems beyond those used by conventional cannabis operations.

LIZ CRAIN is a fiction writer and the author of *Food Lover's Guide to Portland*, editor of *True Portland: The Unofficial Guide for Creative People*, and coauthor of *Toro Bravo: Stories. Recipes. No Bull.* and *Hello! My Name is Tasty: Global Diner Favorites from Portland's Tasty Restaurants*. A longtime writer on Pacific Northwest food and drink, her writing has appeared in *Lucky Peach*, *Food & Wine*, *The Sun Magazine*, *The Progressive*, and the *Guardian*. She is also editor and publicity director at Hawthorne Books as well as co-organizer of the annual Portland Fermentation Festival.